Between the Lines

Christianity for Misfit Christians

John Carter

Between the Lines: Christianity for Misfit Christians

By John Carter

ISBN: 978-0-9831667-0-2

Library of Congress Control Number: 2010917323

Published in Clearwater, Florida, USA

All Scripture quotations in this publication are based on the World English Bible (which is an update of the 1901 American Standard Version) and its Messianic Edition, which are in the public domain. Keep scripture free: http://ebible.org/.

Diamond photo © Ioana Davies (Drutu) - Fotolia.com. Used by permission.

Lantern photo by Pradeep Prakash, www.pradeepclicks.com. Used by permission.

While all the stories are true, people's names have been changed throughout this book.

Website: WWW.MISFITCHRISTIAN.COM

CONTENTS

Introduction

I believe that many of us have become Company Men, who abdicate our hearts and dreams to mere habituation and expectation. Regretfully, most companies, churches and families of origin lie in the ranks of Companies. Is life anywhere to be found between the ranks and files all around us, or must we settle for a coordinate on the grid?

In 2009, pollster George Barna asked people how they would categorize themselves: Casual Christians, Captive Christians, Mormons, Jews, Pantheists, Muslims and Skeptics. Two-thirds of Americans replied casual: faith in moderation and generally living a Christian life. 16% replied captive: focused on Biblical, absolute moral and spiritual truth.[1] If you are a "Casual Christian," then there's a good chance I'm writing to you.

Many "captives" might dismiss the "casuals" as, well, casual: ho-hum, whatever, God-in-moderation. But there's a question here: Is a Christian "casual" because he is busy or not-radical or what? Or could she be in a place that doesn't allow creativity and originality to shine?

If *all* the people who said, "I'm a Christian" suddenly started to live out their God-given dreams in the freedom Jesus promised, I think it could be a scandal in every church in the country, a really good one. And if good news like that spread like a scandal, well, that would be...amazing. Wonderful. A miracle, really.

I hope this little book gives you momentary pause from the hurry-scurry of life. Perhaps you will enjoy the stories. They may give you ideas and inspiration to live a fuller life. I hope that it will refresh and brighten your eyes for God and the people around you, and that you can and will fully embrace and live the only life you've been given—yours

May God give you the dreams of his heart and may all your dreams come true.

John Carter, December 2010

Called but not Chosen

Dreams

"If you could be anywhere, doing anything, with anyone, what would that be? What is it that makes you passionate?"

"Well, if I could, I would...but I couldn't do *that*. I'm too busy."

I have asked hundreds of people that question—friends, students, coworkers—and I found that most people aren't living their dreams. Oddly, I also keep hearing the same answer from Christians, who profess faith in an all-powerful God.

If we asked a random sample of Christians, "What is it that you do, that makes your heart sing?" the collection of answers might be the envy of any church. And if we asked them, "Can you do that thing in your present church, family, and work?" Frequently, they answer, "No." We could then ask, "Why not?", "What are you doing today with little to no enthusiasm?", and "Why are you doing all those things that don't matter to you and missing the life you hear God calling you to?"

Some people are isolated from traditional church programs by financial burdens, caregiving, or social ostracism. How do *they* live out their hearts' desires?

Christians who desire to live lives like those of Christ and the early Christians are often frustrated by half-heartedly working at the limited outlets presented to them, rather than doing the things they love. Asking these questions could reshape our lives, ministries, and churches if we listened thoughtfully to the answers and acted on them with intention. We might start a revolution.

I feel like the apostle Paul when he said, "I am again in the pains of childbirth for you" to the Galatian church, which was busy rulemaking itself into bondage.[1]

I ache for us all to be fully birthed out of bondage and into the freedom of Christ.

Illusions

At his inauguration as Governor of Alabama in January 1963, George Wallace proclaimed his illusion of freedom. "...I say...segregation today...segregation tomorrow...segregation forever." [2]

On April 12, 1963, eight optimistic Birmingham clergymen, Protestant, Jewish and Catholic, wrote a "Call for Unity" against the anti-segregation marches in their city.[3]

On the same day, Good Friday, Bull Connor's Birmingham police arrested Martin Luther King for demonstrating without a permit.[4] A few days later on May 3, police attacked people with dogs and fire hoses in the streets of the "Tragic City." In September of that year, a KKK bomb killed four little girls inside the 16th Street Baptist Church.[5]

From his cell in April, Dr. King wrote a blistering refutation of "Unity." His *Letter from a Birmingham Jail* comments on the comfortable relationship between churches and the status quo of their cultures:

> But the judgment of God is upon the church as never before. If today's church does not recapture the sacrificial spirit of the early church, it will lose its authenticity, forfeit the loyalty of millions, and be dismissed as an irrelevant social club with no meaning for the twentieth century. Every day I meet young people whose disappointment with the church has turned into outright disgust.[6]

He fought racism. But they also apply equally well to the Pharisees of Jesus' time (who reduced their faith from relationships to rules), and to the popes of Martin Luther's time (who usurped God in the pursuit of their own power, wealth, and glory). When we ignore injustice, they apply to us. They also apply when we ignore sacrifice, service, valor and talent.

Like deluded Pharisees and popes before us, we often overlook or suppress (in the name of unity) the amazing gifts of God embodied in *every* Christian. Churches, it seems, are institutions of the status quo. I too, every day meet young people who passionately want to serve God and are frustrated by church responses that range from blank stares to "you can't do that" to outright opposition. And their disillusionment with the church has turned into outright disgust.

Most pastors, when surveyed by the Barna Research Group in 2002, believed that they did an above-average job in everything except fundraising.[7] Well, they can't *all* be above average.

Barna's 2006 surveys showed that pastors consistently overestimated the spiritual well-being of their congregations. How many people said that God is the top priority of their life? Pastors said, on average, 70 percent. The actual number reported by the people? 23 percent.[8] Let's call it The Preachers' Illusion. 77% of the people sitting in pews just aren't that excited about God, but no one knows it? *Really?*

Most televangelists excel at fundraising. Unfortunately, their drumbeat—we're doing fine, send more money—has become the perceived face of Christianity. Meanwhile, the decades-long exodus from traditional mainline churches continues.

Christians and churches are often perceived, accurately and inaccurately, as focused only on politics, gay-bashing, making war on culture, making war on other countries, antifeminist, hypocritical, arrogant, and judgmental. Over and over, the groundswell of this image/reality problem is reported by the under-30 people. We have a problem right now, and in the future it will get worse.[9]

It will get worse *unless* we change, starting with the man or woman we see in the mirror. Our cultures, customs and choices have institutionalized many of us, but we are only a decision away from starting to living out the dreams, passions, and gifts that God has given us. We need to jettison the illusion that everything's just fine.

We need a Reformation.

Quitting

"Now the LORD said to Abram, "Get out of your country, and from your relatives, and from your father's house, to the land that I will show you."
— Genesis 12:1

I was tired of sermons; I'd heard them before. When I walked into the Christian bookstores, the titles were all reruns. Church business meetings were never about the business of God and people; they were about buildings and budgets. God help us; one meeting was devoted to fixing the leaking steeple...[A]

Church people seemed more interested in studying their FAQs than in seeking their own questions and answers. Some of the big ones seemed to be missing at both corporate and personal levels; for example, "Do our/does my budget and calendar reflect the biblical values we are/I am claiming to believe?"

Committee meetings seemed mighty similar to the meetings I was in while working as an engineer for the Army in the missile business. Some of the nicest people I knew were not yet Christians, but his light shone in them. Sadly, some of the meanest people I knew were already Christians.

I should have done it sooner, but I quit. I quit looking at churches in America today as exemplars of Christian community, and started seeking it on my own. I quit listening to the teachings of people, and started listening for the voice of God in the spaces between their words. I quit reading the Bible expecting to find doctrines on salvation, justification, and sanctification, and started reading the texts just as they were written, expecting God's voice to show me what I needed to know and experience. I lowered my expectations of churches, and raised my expectations of God.

Abram lived retired in the city-state of Ur and minded his own busi-

---

[A] I mischievously proposed, in all seriousness, that we just tear it down as an unnecessary distraction. They fixed it.

ness.   While he rested on the banks of the Euphrates River in present-day Iraq, the land of his ancestors, God interrupted his life by saying, "Get up, and let's go. Leave your family and friends. I'll show you where we're going. I will bless you." Abram got up and went, and the rest of his story is the beginning of our story as Christians. The entire history of Israel and Christianity begins with one old man quitting.

Quitting changed Abram's life. Quitting changed my life. I've found things along the way that I hope will change yours.

Chosen?

"For you are a chosen race, a royal priesthood, his workmanship, created in Messiah Jesus for good works, which God prepared before that we would walk in them."
   – 1 Peter 2:9, Ephesians 2:10

God, the master craftsman, created great beauty inside you with which you can bless others. That's really amazing. But even more amazing is the idea that good works were created, designed, for you.   He didn't make you to fit some eternal generic identity/job/ministry description;[B] he wrote the "identity description" around who you are, what you do, and why you want to be and do it.

What we find in most modern institutional churches is a menu of opportunities to share that beauty and be appropriately appreciated for who we are. In bigger churches, the menu is usually bigger either in variety, scale or both. But—and this is the key point—*all* of these menus are designed before you arrive, and they are common denominators existing within the leadership population of that institution. To put it painfully, they serve the *present* market within the church, not the *future* market with you included.

[B] For example, the popular "Five-fold ministry" cookie-cutter.

Even more painfully, The Preachers' Illusion suggests that the menu may not even serve its present market very well: 77% of it, in fact. For many of the incumbents (but not all), this is fine. But for new, different arrivals, it can lead to a church life of relentless futility; trying to express the love and passion in one's heart through a one-size-fits-some strainer.[C] God calls us to him and his great redeeming works in this world, but we can remain unchosen by our own team.

Someone said that everyone's the three big fears are death, aloneness, and irrelevance. To be unchosen is to be alone and irrelevant; isn't that death? We find ourselves alone in the crowd, surrounded by a swirl of activity by seemingly-cheerful people with seemingly-meaningful lives. We want to scream, we want to escape this hell, but we don't know how.[D]

Yes

I believe that God's workmanship in people is like water. It desires to find an outlet, even if it's frozen, diverted, or dammed up (even damned by others as heresy and rebellion...but we'll talk more about that later). Will we let it?

A civil engineer told me that 90% of civil engineering is based on the fact that water always flows downhill (surely he exaggerated.) But he's onto something; look at the amount of drainage around any construction project. All ditches slope downhill. You can dig holding ponds, run ditches, bury culverts, build bridges, set pump and pipe networks...but the water always levels itself before trying to go downhill.

One of the ideas introduced through the internet is "crowdsourc-

---

[C] Some churches even make it abundantly clear that new arrivals are welcome, but not their ideas on what *else* the church should be doing.

[D] For a musical expression of this, listen to Bebo Norman's "Pull me out," http://www.youtube.com/watch?v=K3YwDjbVq9Q

ing." When millions of people with computers, information (video, music, text, etc.), and brains connect with each other, we get incredibly bright, thoughtful environments. Youtube, Wikipedia, Limewire and even the Firefox web browser are exemplars of crowdsourcing done well. Crowdsourcing gives us more information and choices than ever before in history (wisdom, of course, remains priceless).

The crowds of God-given but un-released gifts and passions in this world can easily flow into all the low places of this world *if* we loose them from institutional holding ponds. I'm suggesting that the power of God loosed in that way is not only greater than what is currently dammed up, but in fact what he had in mind in the first place, when he scattered passionate Jesus-people all over the Roman Empire.

Fear

But often we're afraid to journey along new rivers, unwilling to accept our own freedom and the responsibility that goes with it. Why are we afraid?

"Fear" is specific; it has:
- *Magnitude*, as in "I'm terrified..." or "I'm a little uneasy.."
- An *object*, as in "...of the dark..." or "...of other people.."
- A *consequence*, as in "...because I'll be hurt..." or "they'll hate me..."
- A *reason*, as in, "...like the night the dog bit me." Or "...like someone did to me before."

Fear's object is about the question, "*What* am I afraid of?"

It's common for people to talk about being *stressed* about their work, families, and churches. Behind that kind of stress,[E] though, isn't there an edge of fear? Stress is just a politically correct word

---

[E] I'm only talking here about lifestyle and culture-driven situations, not poverty, war or similar situations.

for fear; "I'm stressed" sounds less vulnerable than "I'm afraid." But *stress* is a generalized and non-directional word, as in "This meeting stresses me out." We hide behind *stressed* and sometimes even make a virtue of it. We avoid the disturbing questions, "*Who* am I afraid of?" and "*What* am I afraid they will do to me?" and "*How* will some part of me die if they do it?"

So the socially unwelcome question for stressed-out churches and Christians is, "If you aren't living out your God-given dreams, who is it that you're afraid will make some part of you dead, alone or irrelevant?"

I believe the great unspoken sin in our churches today is that too many of us condemn and reject the ones who dance and sing to the songs of *God*, not the march of a institution's status quo. Fear of rejection is the rope than binds us to the stake of other men's dreams, instead of God's. Fear of others' condemnation is the noose around our necks that tightens when we walk away from the stake.

Other men's dreams may offer us the rope, but *only* our acceptance of it leads to bondage. In a ghastly kind of barter, we accept the noose to purchase acceptance.

Caged

Every teacher and coach knows the frustration of trying to connect with a group and failing. Sometimes it's the teacher; I have days when I can't tap my enthusiasm for the subject, and it kills the intimacy between me and the class. Other days, the class is tough: impervious to jokes, icebreakers, questions, passion—everything. Sometimes, none of us really want to be there which isn't pretty, and some days it's an architectural problem.

Any room or building that focuses attention on only a few people takes us toward a fool's-gold cage of performance with lighting, drama, and entertainers, representation instead of reality, and seem-ing instead of be-ing.

A typical proscenium stage has three walls: a backdrop and wings on each side. The front of the stage is open (it's called "the fourth wall") so that the audience and performers can see each other and interact. Sometimes, though, it's as though a real fourth wall, invisible and frustrating, is there at the front of the stage.

I saw a pastor, a teacher actually, locked behind the fourth wall one day. He stretched out, trying to connect to the hearts of the audience and failing completely. It was sickening, because I was sitting right where that invisible wall was and saw both sides.

I could see the horrible reality of that glass wall—*both* sides held it up. Something in that man's love of speaking to a big audience and avoidance of intimacy was holding it up from his side, and that audience's love of being spoken to (versus spoken with) and avoidance of intimacy was holding it up from the other. It was a tragedy, a sick agreement to share a room but not a journey. In all the time we were at that church, the wall never came down. Slowly and sadly, I realized that they chose alienation, but called it inspiration. [F]

The Sick and the Dead

"Hope deferred makes the heart sick, but when longing is fulfilled, it is a tree of life."
— Proverbs 13:12

When we cage ourselves and others with the expectations and limitations of a scripted life, we end up in a kind of dreary hope-deferred world. You see it sometimes in middle-aged couples. The jobs are solid, retirement's ahead, the kids are in college. Church and club activities occupy their timeslots. All the questions are known, and most are answered. Vacations are scheduled and taken. Nothing unexpected is expected. The cage door is closed and locked from the inside.

[F] See also the song "Limelight," by Rush, *Moving Pictures*, 1981; http://www.youtube.com/watch?v=0mwiURyX2B4.

(At least, until the unexpected comes to shatter the expected. Look at the formerly mild and peaceful hobbits of *The Lord of the Rings* when an evil reality arises.)

And what of chance and courage? What of valor? Are they so distant as to be unreachable? Are they even beyond desire? Has the desire to *matter* been smothered by habit and comfort? That is truly sad. It may be true for you. That caged-up living-deadness is the real thing—a sick heart—to be frightened of. God, help us; let not your dreams pass beyond our ken. We are the children of the King of Kings, and *that does not have to be our fate.*

Uncaged

I taught short technical courses for several years and loved it. My passion for missiles, technology, and the possibilities that open up when people choose to pool their talents in pursuit of worthy goals showed. I was good at communicating the information and inspiring students. Most of all, I *liked* the students; I *liked* the dialog with them. The "I don't know" point came in those dialogues, and I loved how they fed each other's, and my own, creativity. It was humanity.

I spent a lot of time out in the middle of the class. The fourth wall was my mortal enemy. I hated the lectern. It was a cage that threatened us.

The best meetings I've ever been in were all in rooms less than 20'x20' with several whiteboards, lots of markers, a small table, scattered papers, and people correcting and adding to sketches and diagrams. We solved problems, and came up with life and creation that way.

The room was full of oxygen for questions, dialog, and relationships. There wasn't room for a cage. A fourth wall was impossible, because we were sideways—face to face with each other. Life in Christian community wants to be like that. The reality of our humanity is this: we believe best those things in which we participate most.

When the church experience is *ecclesia semper reformanda*, "the church always re-forming," we have exploration, discovery, and life.

The Invisible Church

King's Birmingham heart-cry climaxes with these words:

> "Is organized religion too inextricably bound to the status quo to save our nation and the world? Perhaps I must turn my faith to the inner spiritual church, the church within the church, as the true *ekklesia* and the hope of the world."

The apostle Paul wrote from prison to the church at Philippi. Throughout his letter he proclaims the positive in that community but notes, "with tears, many live as enemies of the cross of Christ." [10] Like these two prison authors, I can't remain silent while people are silently, or not-so-silently, screaming for release.

I turn for hope to the individuals who find the person and teachings of Jesus attractive. Some of them are in churches. Some have left churches in sheer frustration. Some have never set foot in a church. These are the true Church, the *ekklesia* as Jesus called it in the Greek language of his time and place. They are largely "inner" and invisible in part because of that 70/23 gap between those with pulpits and those without. But they are God-given to change this challenging world. Finally, I am turning for hope to the not-yet-Christians, imploring them to give us another chance to share with them a living Jesus, who has a place and a hope for *them*.

Join me. Please. It can be wonderful and lonely out here in the Invisible Church. We can find each other if we look, and listen to God's whispers to our hearts.

And now...

Like the "Validation"^G video, in which our hero praises people as he validates their parking tickets, let's hear some Good News. Let's eavesdrop on the stories and metaphors that give us four truths to live by, using some very old words to renew ones we already know: image, church, disciple, servant.

---

^G This is an amazing little video about a guy who just liked to see people smile; what if *we* did this? See http://www.youtube.com/watch?v=Cbk980jV7Ao.

Imago Dei

Shaped

"God created man in his own image. In God's image he created him; male and female he created them."
  – Genesis 1:27

Michelangelo left a sculpture[A] of the disciple Matthew, the former tax collector (a Jewish traitor to the Romans) unfinished. The statue's face looks toward heaven, his body still partially submerged in stone. You see the ragged places where the sculptor is chiseling away and revealing the man from his native rock. The eyes are full of longing as he seeks his creator, while being revealed by his creator, reveled in by his creator.

The sculpture has expression, personality, and depth. He wears clothes and carries a tablet under his left arm. He's husky and athletic. He's shaped like his sculptor. And he's made from rock—the earth. Like Adam, whose very name means "earth." [B]

We're made in God's image, but we're unfinished. We're longing, seeking, being revealed by our sculptor, and being reveled in by one who said, "Let us make man in *our* image." And the thing is, unlike Michelangelo and *St. Matthew*, he's alive and still sculpting us in real time, all the time.

Early Christians who spoke Latin referred to *"Imago Dei,"* the image of God. Our ways are like his, distorted but recognizable. Emerging.

————

[A] The statue is called "St. Matthew." See it at
http://www.backtoclassics.com/gallery/michelangelo/stmatthew1/.

[B] A man named "dirt?" For a gardener or civil engineer, soil is a bed and foundation for life and glorious creation.

Like the saying, "That apple didn't fall very far from the tree." Different, still-forming, yet the same in recognizable ways.

Igloos in Florida

"For I know the plans I have for you," declares the LORD, "plans to prosper you and not to harm you, plans to give you hope and a future."
—Jeremiah 29:11

I frequently realize that something I'm doing or believing isn't what I really want to do or believe. I keep finding out that my "answers" need to be revised, because they just don't make sense to me or they aren't what God has written and is saying to me.

So I was watching a program on TV about hurricanes, and they showed a slow-motion video of a concrete roof tile, just like the ones on our roof, hitting a standard steel-shutter-covered window at a paltry 45 miles per hour. It didn't penetrate, but the shutter dented far enough to shatter the glass. You can imagine the scene and the sting. I'm starting to wonder if I really want tiles on my roof if they're going to go raining sideways through my neighbors' houses.

I'm also starting to wonder if tiles *ever* made sense here in Florida. You can see them all over northern Europe, the Mediterranean, Spain; major places in our architectural genealogy. One great reason for those (mostly clay) tiles is, they work and they're fireproof. But none of those places have hurricanes.

I thought, "That's like when I do things that aren't really me, the person God created me to be; they're borrowed or superimposed on my real identity. Those career and personality choices, hobbies and hangouts may have suited the people I acquired them from. But sometimes I put these things on that don't suit my face, frame or environment."

So I got to thinking about a little more absurd and elaborate example than roof tiles. Maybe igloos?

Well, you *could* build an igloo in Florida. I think you'd want to start off with one big enough to live in. Then, you'd want to build a sort of cage of refrigeration pipes, with a nice big cooling unit to bring it down to, say, about 0 degrees Fahrenheit. (Got lots of money in your bank account? Yes? Good; you'll need it for the utility bills.) Then you'd want to somehow get some snow and pack it all around them, maybe about a foot thick. How, exactly, would you do that? That would give you your very own, nice unique home in sunny Florida. You might be quite proud of the year-round cooling.

An igloo would be silly even by Florida's silly-to-sublime architectural standards. People might think you were crazy. Except—and this is the *really* crazy part—what if a whole bunch of people had igloos here? In fact, what if there were a whole igloo industry, and maybe even a Church of Igloo, and lots of cultural skepticism (that's a nice phrase for prejudice) about people who lived in non-igloo houses?

It would still be crazy. Common doesn't make anything normal.

But isn't that what we do, individually and collectively? Our cultures and families of origin do a lot to set our courses early in life. Those courses are always mixtures of good and bad, aren't they? A support-our-boy's-education family might also be very driven; a "whatever" culture might not grasp a girl's need for advanced college education and professional mentors. And so it is that that boy and girl glimpse their God-created identity and calling only through a haze of assumptions, prejudices, and ignorance.

The beliefs that comprise your relationship with God, however they actually influences your life, are a part of you. "Things are the way they are, because they *got* that way." Things didn't get that way without reason; they weren't random, and many may have made sense in their time and culture. But some of them are probably igloos in Florida, for you.

Here's what I'd like to know:
- What's that thing in your heart?
- Who put it there?
- What are you going to do with it?

We can read plenty about who God is, ask him who we are, and compare his answers to the things we've believed thus far. In church cultures, we do a lot of that first one: study God's word. The next two (who are we and what do we *really* believe?) are just as foundational, but we tend not to do them. I don't know why.

"The purpose of life isn't to arrive sedately at the grave with a well-preserved corpse, but rather to slide in, sideways, bent and battered, yelling, 'Wow! What a ride!'" I saw that painted on the back of a motorcycle racer's trailer, and I loved it.

I want to finish having lived *all* of this life I've been given. *Lived.*

Diamonds

"Children of God...seen as lights in the world, holding up the word of life."
  – Philippians 2:15b-16a

What does a human made in the *imago dei* look like? Well, for starters, since Jesus says he's light,[1] perhaps we look like light as well. Or maybe, a diamond.[c]

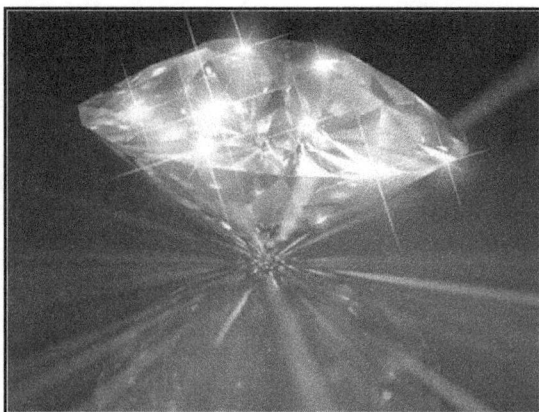

_____

[c] A diamond is made of carbon, the same stuff that is 18% of you...and by far the dominant solid material in you. Almost all the rest is oxygen and hydrogen – air and water. But that's another message for another time...

18

A diamond has no light of its own, but if you shine a laser into a diamond (red is fine, but green is eye-popping), the room fills with brilliant points of light, like stars in red or green. The pattern alters with every tiny change in the angle between the laser and the diamond.

The light shines *on* the diamond's surfaces and is reflected at different angles, but it also shines *into* the diamond's heart and is refracted (bent) into many new directions inside the diamond. Each new ray of light reflects internally and eventually emerges to become another point in our laser constellation, producing a pattern unique to that diamond that changes when the diamond moves.

If there were white-light lasers, those refracted-prism rays of light would be in all the colors of the rainbow. All around, all colors, all glorious.

Maybe that's like what scripture means when it says we will shine like stars or lights in the world.[2] We have no light except the one that God shines on us, but we reflect and refract that light in a thousand unique directions and colors.

Scripture talks about a God who places every star in the sky and knows each by name.[3] The same God shines his light on and through us; he designed and named all of our ways just as he named each star. Like all of creation, we were made to be beautiful and wonderful. He intended his people to be even more awe-inspiring than desert skies, unrecognizably crowded with lights.

We are made of mere carbon, the stuff of pencils and coal mines and diamonds. The difference between us and a lump of coal is the shaping hand of a Creator, a good God, who ordained beauty in *all* things from the very beginning, who said it was *all* good.

Light

"Christ is our life."
 – Colossians 3:4

What if the Creator not only shone through us, but put some of his own light inside us? What if he said, "Let there be light" not only in the universe, but inside every human?[4] Then what?

I lit a kerosene hurricane lantern and put it at the end of a lonely road. Just a little lantern; the flame was maybe a half inch tall. Then I got in the car—I wish I'd just walked and *felt* the distance— and started driving away from it. I could see it receding in the rear-view mirror as I drove. Further and further, smaller and smaller, until I ran out of road something over a mile away and could still see it, one little yellow dot, scintillating slightly in the blackness. Somewhere over there, far away, was a warm little circle of light and warmth. I could imagine a few friends gathered around it, talking, smiling, and warming by the flame.

Just a little flame. How far away could it be seen in a really, really dark place?

We *are* the lanterns. Jesus said, "Let your light shine."[5] In fact, he said, let your light shine like a city on a hill, or a lamp on a lamp stand, and for crying out loud, don't stick it under a bucket.

What if our light was visible far, far beyond our imagining? The little lantern couldn't see me, because it was far away, in sooty darkness, night-blinded by its own light. But I saw it. If I needed hope and encouragement, if I needed some sense of direction, the little flame would be with me for the long, stumbling trudge back to its glowing circle.

And most of the time, the little lantern would believe that it glowed in vain, all alone.

What if we hid our light? Perhaps the world around us would look...the way it looks. Dark. Disoriented.

Broken

"...it is God who said, 'Light will shine out of darkness,' who has shone in our hearts, to give the light of the knowledge of the glory of God in the face of Jesus the Messiah. But we have this treasure in clay vessels, that the exceeding greatness of the power may be of God, and not from ourselves. Though our outward man is decaying, yet our inward man is renewed day by day."
    – 2 Corinthians 4:6-7, 16b

I was singing my heart out at a worship gathering in the spring of 2007, eyes closed, when I saw a vision of a broken and reassembled clay pot with gaps between the shards. A brilliant white light shone out through the cracks. In fact, the light was so bright and hot that it slowly ablated the edges of the cracks away. The pot could not contain the light and was consumed from the inside out by the fire—and the pot was glad. It grew closer to me, as well, while being transformed into pure light. It was beautiful.

The pot is each of us, designed to be beautiful and to contain great beauty. But we come into the world already cracked—self-centered, demanding, and desiring others to serve us. Swiftly, we acquire additional cracks: wounds. We sin against others and in so doing wound ourselves. Others sin against us and hurt us deeply. Soon, as "children" (of any age), we resemble that shattered clay pot. The sins and wounds are real and numerous: rape, religion, larceny, murder, abortion, envy, selfishness, ambition, gossip, boasting, mercilessness, greed, adultery, death, abandonment, loneliness, irrelevance. We are cracked, perpetrators and victims alike.

Try as we might to "keep it together" and to fix and ignore them, our cracks show on the outside. We patch and mismatch; we paint over the holes, but it's only exchanging lies and demons for more of the same. When I was small, I patched with smarts, manipulation, and humor. When I was afraid of the dark and felt like prey, I patched by choosing to be a predator: ambitiously walking over opponents and using the not-so-opposed people all the way.

God puts his light *in* us, and it will not be hidden. Soon, sometimes all of a sudden, the cracks and flaws are on display because of the pure light within us. When reborn, we experience the Holy Counselor who shows us our sins[6] and gives freedom from them.[7] We see them and our souls shout, "Hypocrite!" Other people see them and shout, "Hypocrite!" Like Adam, we keep trying to cover our cracks with fig leaves that don't cover and don't last.[D] We patch holes with more self-made clay. We are ashamed...others shame us...

But the cracks we're trying to cover are simply the places where God is growing within us and out of us. We already know that healing is found in uncovering our sins.[8] The reality is the eternal light within; the deception is that the clay fragments, which are being consumed, can or should be reassembled into the original pot. What if we agreed with God to let the light grow at the expense of the clay?

Song sing of it; songs like Brian Doerksen's *Refiner's Fire* and Hillsong

---

[D] Genesis 3:6-11 gives us the silly picture of people making clothes from fig leaves sewn together. They're somewhat bigger than my hand, but *really*...don't those things itch?

United's *Inside Out* are anthems that cry out for God's transforming fire in our lives. Doerksen's *You Shine* proclaims God's courage and strength in us to pursue his light before us. We sing of our ultimate end in the last verse of *Amazing Grace*; "...bright, shining as the sun..." Sometimes tears flow; tears at the loss of our clay, and joy of gain from our Light.

As God transforms our flaws in his light, they become exhibitions of redeeming grace and his power in our lives, and they glorify him. If no one sees the evil we have done, then how can they see God overcoming that evil through the transformation of our hearts?

> "Now the Lord is the Spirit and where the Spirit of the Lord is, there is liberty. But we all, with unveiled face beholding as in a mirror the glory of the Lord, are transformed into the same image from glory to glory, even as from the Lord, the Spirit. You are our letter, written in our hearts, known and read by all men; being revealed that you are a letter of the Messiah, served by us, written not with ink, but with the Spirit of the living God; not in tablets of stone, but in tablets that are hearts of flesh."
> – *2 Corinthians 3:17-18 and 3:2-3*

Unveiled faces...cracked pots...transformed into his Glory. Jesus tore open the veil in the temple; he's asking to tear open the veil over your face. Has our desire to keep and cover our cracks been greater than our desire to be light in the world?

Like the lamp, your light-leaking cracks can be seen over a long distance; further than you may think. The pastor from my teen years still shines to me, 30 years and many miles later. I heard two stories this last year about times I'd blessed someone over 15 years ago—I didn't remember it; they sure did. Like a city on a hill, so are you.[9]

Shining, part 1

There's a saying in the South: "That boy, he's the spittin' image of his daddy." I never understood what spitting had to do with an image, until I learned that the phrase is a countrified contraction of the phrase "Spirit and image." So if someone says, "That boy is in the spirit and image of his Daddy," I know that he looks like his daddy outside *and* inside.

Christians are being transformed daily by his Spirit within us, to radiate more and more of God's Spirit and look more and more like his Image. After all, Jesus didn't say only that he came to light the world, to lead people out of their darkness (he promptly healed a blind man, underlining his point). He also said, early in his ministry and to many thousands of people, "*You* are the light of the world [that] can't be hidden. Let your light shine before men [so] that they may glorify your Father who is in heaven."[10]

There's another old saying: "Your life may be the only bible some people ever read." The apostle Peter counseled that we should live our lives so that even our deeds persuade unbelievers to praise God. If we really *are* created in the image of God, re-created by Jesus, and we cohabit these bodies with his Spirit, then don't we have the opportunity and ability to actually live out those sayings?

There was a man named Daniel who lived in present-day Iraq and Iran around 600 B.C. As a child, he was kidnapped from his home in Israel, but promoted by kings to lead great (pagan) empires three times in his long life. Never once did he seek office, but always he served. He's best remembered for his "Daniel in the Lions' Den" experience.

Anyone remember how he got there in the first place?

One hundred twenty-two bureaucrats schemed to undermine Daniel's upcoming promotion over them (he was already in the top three of the 123). Every one of them and the king who intended to promote Daniel to run the kingdom for him knew that he was trustworthy, incorruptible, attentive to his job, and Godly. The schemers knew that men who serve a God higher than themselves endanger the schemes of other men.

Well, it's hard to indict someone for being a model civil servant. They tricked the king, through his vanity, into signing a 30-day decree: "No one can pray except to me, Darius! If they do, I'll throw them in the lions' den." Then they outed Daniel for his daily prayers to God. The king was mortified, but at that time his decrees were irrevocable, even by him.

After a sleepless night of fasting, the king got up at dawn and hurried to the lions' den. When he approached the den, he cried out, "Daniel, servant of the living God, is your God, whom you serve continually, able to deliver you from the lions?"[11]

The painting is entitled, "Daniel's answer to the king."

Daniel was arrested, condemned and then vindicated for being faithful to God. He let God's light shine so brightly through him among the unbelievers that even the king (the absolute monarch of all he surveyed) "glorified God."[E]

The old question is, "If you were on trial for your life, charged with being a Christian, would there be enough evidence to convict you?" Many would plead guilty. Police and prosecutors would seek evidence. They would ask, "Are you concealing evidence? Are you hiding the God-part of your actions under dire or even not-so-dire circumstances?"[12] Our answer is, too often, yes.

Perhaps if I quit hiding the evidence of God's spirit in me or even

---

[E] You probably noticed that "nice guys" don't habitually keep a den of lions handy for enemies. The quotes are from 1 Peter 2:11-12 in the New Testament.

claiming his light is my own, people would see him through me. Like Daniel. Now *that* would be the spittin' image of Jesus. *That* would be letting his light shine.

Shining, part 2

Mohandas Gandhi searched for the roots of violence. He called these acts of passive violence, by societies as well as individuals.[13] He wasn't a Christian. But is there anything on this list that Jesus would disagree with?
- Wealth without work
- Pleasure without conscience
- Knowledge without character
- Commerce without morality
- Science without humanity
- Worship without sacrifice
- Politics without principle
- Rights without responsibilities

Could the opposite of this list resemble some parts of *Imago Dei*?
- Wealth from work
- Pleasure with conscience
- Knowledge with character
- Commerce with morality
- Science with humanity
- Worship with sacrifice
- Politics with principle
- Rights with responsibilities

If you met someone who embodied these behaviors, might you recognize glimmers of God's wisdom and justice?

The thing about *imago dei* is that God designed us to be like him. He hasn't forgotten his design for mankind or forgotten his craftsmanship of you and me, and he hasn't left us in some void where all we have is written teachings. We have his Spirit living inside of us to help us understand and apply them.

If and when we listen, we sometimes hear God's whispers into our hearts. And he hasn't finished yet.

Some people love to live out careers of moral commerce, doing business away from sweatshops and wage slavery of any type. Others might be passionate advocates for justice for the helpless, comforters for the wounded, or sacrificial, intercessory worshippers for mankind. The variety is endless, because God isn't limited to a list of 7 or 12 or 40 or some other holy number of ways to shine his light through us. No two sets of fingerprints or DNA are alike, and no two sets of callings are alike. There's no scriptural mandate or reason that they be.

Iranaeus, a 2nd century leader in what is now Lyon, France, wrote, "The glory of God is man fully alive, and the life of man is the vision of God." [14] The Creator is most glorified by his creation living in full accord with his design.

Gandhi also said, "Be the change you wish to see." So you want God to light the world, save the sinners, or establish justice for the poor and oppressed? Well, what Christian doesn't want something like that, at least in the abstract? So should you try to work off that laundry list of should-dos? But that's work without heart. Mark Twain said, "Work consists of what a body is *obliged* to do." But if you let your God-given passions be seen and heard far and wide, well, that's hardly work, but it's a lot of heart. The rest of Twain's proverb is, after all, "Play consists of what a body is *not* obliged to do."

Be the change. Play. Shine.

We Shine

So we're each one-of-a-kind but all of the God-kind. Diamonds and lanterns and pots, oh my! [F] No two alike; how will we arrange them? Won't there be chaos?

[F] My apologies to Dorothy in *The Wizard of Oz*.

A few dozen of us gathered for worship on Sunday morning. We handed out about a half-dozen laser pointers, several red, several green. We told people to shine them on their diamond rings if they had them. The room was filled with dancing, changing light. It was beautiful. It was alive. We were beautiful. We were alive.

The lasers are just a simplified and metaphorical version of God's light, which is the life-light of men, brought by Jesus.[15] His light is brighter. His light is white, which contains *all* colors. So try to imagine a room filled with people-sized diamonds, each individually illuminated by a brilliant multicolor laser, dancing. As great as the beauty that God put in each and every one of us is, that beauty multiplies when we come together. Add people, multiply effects.

If we believe that God is the light-giver, can we also believe he will adjust the lights to suit himself? If we can believe that, we can relax and quit trying to fix the "chaos" in and between other people.

If we come to accept that we really are created in God's image, with his design and beauty inbuilt, and if we openly live and speak that truth, people around us will see God. Then, when he opens their eyes to the inexplicable grace right in front of them, they can come to know him as well. And "they" become part of "us." The "we" of our little worlds gets just a little bigger.

Next...

And since we're going to quit building igloos in Florida, who is "we," anyway?

Ekklesia

(at a large church in Virginia, July 2006)

Called Out

"...Messiah also is the head of the assembly, being himself the savior of the body."
— Ephesians 5:23b

The Greek word *ekklesia (ek-lay-SEE-ah)* translated as "church" 77 times in the Bible is the combination of *ek* (out) and *kaleo* (call). The words *agora* and *paneguris* as well as *heorte, koinon, thiasos, suna-goge* and *sunago* also refer to assemblies of people. What's so special about *ekklesia*?

Ekklesia was a political, and not religious, term. In classical Greek, it meant an assembly of citizens summoned to a legislative assembly by a crier. When the Greek city-states found that their governments became too corrupt or oppressive, they called for an *ekklesia*, an assembly outside the civil authority of the city. They literally met outside the city boundaries to collectively talk things over. If enough people refused to accept the existing centralized civil authority, the government would collapse.[1] An ekklesia was what we might call a town hall meeting, but with a lot more bite than our usual Q&A sessions with elected leaders. If a change of management was needed, they would go out, *ekklesia*, go back to town, and resume their usual lives.

We who are Christians are called out from *every*-thing to be part of *some*-thing else. Really, we are summoned to be part of some *One* else, a relationship. We are called out from where we are, called together to strengthen relationships with God and each other, and called back to the world we came from. Called from Ordinary lives to become an Extra-ordinary Body[2] of Christ.

Who is "we?" We are the ones who show up at any given moment for worship, lunch, coffee and bagels, or a sales meeting. We are the subset in any given group, sacred or secular; who are God's and lighted by God. Our sign says, "everybody's welcome, come on in, let's talk, pray" regardless of appearance, transgression, or membership.

Breathing and Walking Together

"...when he, the Spirit of truth, has come, he will guide you into all truth..."
  — John 16:13a

Remember *kaleo*, "called," from ekklesia? During the last Passover meal, Jesus promised that the Holy Spirit, the "Comforter," will live with and in the disciples (we say "spirit," but it is the Greek word is *pneuma*, "breath," as in, creation-breath of God).[3] He calls the Comforter the *para-kletos*, which is a compound of p*ara,* which means "beside," and *kletos (like kaleo meaning* "called"). The Holy Spirit is the "Called-alongside one." He's the air that we share.

Scuba divers breathe using a regulator, which reduces the air pressure from their tank down to the exact pressure needed to breathe at their current depth. A diver doesn't have to think about it; he just breathes normally. Since a regulator is a life-or-death item, it's worth having two. Divers *always* dive with two regs. Not just for themselves; for their dive buddy, too. How far should you be from your buddy? No more than a breath away.

If you run out of air, and you are as close to your buddy as you should be, you snatch your buddy's spare reg and start breathing normally again. Until you can surface, the two of you are sharing one tank of air. Chances are, you'll hold on to him for dear life. And he, you.

The Spirit is called alongside us and enables us to walk beside each other. Even within a breath of each other. And, when we walk with the Spirit inside of us and beside someone else, the result is that they have the *Parakletos* walking beside them in us. We, the called-out (*ekklesia*) ones, are also the called-alongside (*parakletos*) ones. We were called out so that we *can* be called together and called beside. Like scuba divers, we each have air, and sometimes we desperately need to share. Perhaps even quite a bit of the time.

Each person has abilities and limitations, giftings and impairments, blessings and wounds. The "assembly" of all these into one body[4] by the Spirit brings communal good to us. Every assembly is a custom work of his craftsmanship. We limp along together sharing each others' burdens and lightening our own. "A burden shared is a burden halved."

We were created in *Imago Dei*; we form one Body together and are inhabited by the Breath of that Creator. Those two things go together, don't they? Almost as if Body and Breath were designed for each other.

"Each Others" and "One Anothers"

Is *ekklesia* really that important? Does it rank up there with things like good teaching, evangelism, and worship? If we are called to be together, then we might do a check with scripture to find out what it means to live well with one another.

"Do" to one another	**"Don't do" to one another**
Love (at least 7 direct scriptures on this one), Administer true justice, Show kindness, mercy and compassion, especially to those who are downtrodden or poor, Wash feet, Be devoted, Honor, Harmony, Associate with the lowly, Peace, Shared learning, Unity, agreement, Accept, Wait, Equality, Holy kiss, Serve, Humble, Gentle, Patient, forbearing, Carry burdens, Forgiving, Interests of others, Mutual submission, Teach, Admonish, correct, Peace, harmony, Encourage, Hospitality, Confess sins, Pray for.	Think evil, Oppress, Proud, conceited, Pass judgment, Put up stumbling blocks, Provoking, Envying, Selfish ambition, Lie, Slander.

Lest this look like a "to do" list, this is a good time to mention that when, not if, we do these things badly, God's grace is there for us in abundance. "Each man should give what he has decided in his heart to give, not reluctantly or under compulsion...and God is able to make all grace abound to you, so that in all things at all times, having all that you need, you will abound in every good work." [5] *Ekklesia* coerced is not *ekklesia* at all, neither are works coerced works at all. An *ekklesia* is a place where people give and do according to their God-inspired desires to.

I'm just suggesting it's much more foundational than we've traditionally seen in our western, modern, oh-so-independent worldviews.

Who *wouldn't* be attracted to the list on the left? What if how we lived was visible to everyone? If our *ekklesia* looked like the left column, if we learned to live interdependently with each other, would there be *any* energy left for the list on the right? It's happened before.

Writing in 197 A.D., Tertullian of Carthage, in North Africa, recorded how their enemies mocked Christians. "'See,' say they, 'how they love each other!'—for they themselves hate each other; and, 'how ready they are to die for each other!'—for they are more ready to kill each other." [6] That crazy Christianity cult grew and grew; they looked and acted differently from (and behaved better than) anyone else in their culture.

Who *wouldn't* be attracted to that?

Intimacy

Earlier, we spoke of cage-stages and fourth walls. Just as those things help us to imprison each other by a kind of terrible mutual agreement, there are ways we choose freedom. They all help decrease our fear of being uncovered in front of each other of being seen as we really are (like Adam and Eve with their poor fig leaves). This is why I love small rooms, circles, and seating in-the-round, and hate raised lecterns and auditoriums. I have yet to see intimacy, as important as it is to *ekklesia*, in anything other than a circular, level setting.

Have you ever noticed how most church architecture resembles formal buildings like the US Senate, courtrooms and classrooms? That model comes from the Roman Senate: one guy at the rostrum, with a large number of chairs attentively pointed at it. Emperor Constantine imposed it when he declared that his Empire was now Christian.

Winston Churchill said that "We shape our buildings; thereafter they shape us." Once we cast the shape of our assemblies in stone, we're stuck with them. Church buildings are made to focus attention on one man, not to enable conversation and intimacy.[7] Constantine's Senate lurks behind practically every sermon in America today...and we call it "church."

Before

The first few chapters of Acts describe of the very first Christian *ek-klesia*. Before that word even comes up in the narrative, we have a description of the believers that would scream "cult" to our American culture. People gather, learn, eat, and experience grace and healing together. They shared all their possessions with each other, rich and poor. They're in one accord—and scripture implies that everyone lived this way by their own free-will choices, not reluctantly or because someone told them to. [8]

The words used to describe these gatherings are *plēthos* (which means just what it sounds like: a plethora, a plentitude) and *koinōnia (koy-no-NEE-ah)*. *Koinonia* covers a lot of ground. It doesn't mean mere "fellowship," as in a covered dish dinner. It also means communion, communication, contribution, sharing, and participation. Think of a common, shared cup (let's hope no one backwashes). Think of a family made up of peers, not just momma, daddy and the kids.

Jesus called his disciples and followers his brothers and sisters.[9] He meant it.

And then the word *ekklesia* starts to show up throughout the rest of Acts. Somewhere, they go from a common *koinonia* life to being a called-out group of people.

Sound like a cult to you, too? Nope. It's just a community, a Body, living out Christianity, then and now. Normal *and* usual, at least, ordinary and usual unless we let ourselves get hijacked or abandoned. Again.

Humble Assembly

"...the body is one, but has many members...so also is the Messiah. For in one Spirit we were all baptized into one body...and were all given to drink into one Spirit. God has set the members, each one of them, in the body, just as he desired. But God composed the body together, giving more abundant honor to the inferior parts, so that

there should be no division in the body, but that the members should have the same care for one another."
    – 1 Corinthians 12:12-13, 18, 24,25

I'm not very good at jigsaw puzzles. The shapes all look alike to me. I limp along by grouping colors and patterns, and lean heavily on recognizing edges and shapes. Heaven help me if I can't cheat by looking at the picture on the box. And what if a few pieces are missing, or there are a few mixed in from other, similar puzzles? There might be, you know.

Puzzles are designed and printed as a whole, then die-cut by their makers into parts designed to interface and interlock in unique ways. Subtract or force-fit even one,[A] and the picture is incomplete, ruined. A picture comes on the box to show you what it looks like when it's reassembled. If puzzle pieces were alive, what would they say?

"Don't lose me, and don't lose any of my friends, even the ones I haven't seen or touched; we need each other! We're desperate for you to put us *all* together. We want to be a whole picture.

[A] Don't look so pious...surely I'm not the only one who's tried this?

"Besides, it's lonely here. We can't seem to hug up against each other the way we're designed to.

"We tried picking a committee and a chairman to arrange us, but they couldn't see us very well because we're all flat on the table and we can't see each others' shapes at all. Worst of all, we have no idea of what we're supposed to look like or how big we'll be when we are assembled.

"You have a higher point of view; you live in three dimensions and we live in only two. You can see our shapes *and* our insides. You know how we're designed. Will you assemble us? Please?"[B]

"You also, as living stones, are built up as a spiritual house, to be a holy priesthood...you are a chosen race, a royal priesthood, a holy nation, a people of God's own..."[10]

If puzzle pieces have trouble, how much harder is it for us 3-D living stones to assemble each other into a house? No matter how smart or wise we are?

You were made for a purpose, *and* a purpose was made for you. Similarly, purposes are made for assemblies of believers, and those believers are assembled for those purposes. One God, whose ways are higher than ours, designed all people, all purposes, all places, and all assemblies. [11]

Now wouldn't it change our view of the world if we believed that, and were humble enough to understand that we don't have more than a glimpse of the beauty, the *imago dei*, inside each other? But that he sees us all, completely? And that he's a good God, in a good mood, and no one can talk him out of it. [12]

Time

A man walked up to three workers at a construction site. He asked

----

[B] "...as the heavens are higher than the earth, so are my ways higher than your ways..." – God (Isaiah 55:9)

the first, "What are you doing?"

"Laying bricks."

"What are you doing?" he asked the second.

"Building a wall."

He came to the third and asked, "What are you doing?"

"I'm building a cathedral."

As one blogger put it, "How do you build a cathedral? You plant an oak grove, and in a hundred years you have enough wood to build your cathedral, but for a hundred years people are saying your grove is not really a cathedral."[C]

How do you build an *ekklesia*? Take a cathedral worldview. Invest your time, gifts, vulnerability and intimacy in the people God sends to you. Wait on God to grow your saplings into oak trees and your oak trees into cathedrals. Don't assume you'll see the finished work, the destination but instead experience the journey. The journey *is* the destination. [D]

When do you expect your *ekklesia* to look like a "cathedral?" [13]

Each, Every, and One

Sometimes I hear, "May God bless each and every one of you!" It's as though we have a compound word without a concrete idea behind it: eachandeveryone. If I translated that into Southern dialect (my native tongue), it would be "y'all." Somehow the individual gets spread into a sort of fluffy, feel-good collective. I hear it from TV

[C] Andrew Jones, http://www.tallskinnykiwi.com. Used by permission.

[D] This is a much-quoted phrase from John Wimber, founder of the Vineyard church movement. He talked about the perpetual tension between the "now" and the "not-yet" of God's completed work in all the world. But we don't have to figure out the whole scheme; all we have to decide is what to do with today.

preachers, talking to the camera instead of to the people right there in the room with them (Gruesome, really; someone conversing so sincerely to the dead eye of a camera).

In contrast, if we *really* believe that each person is created in the image of God, then "each and every one" has some nice implications.

"Each" is personal, individual, and suggests a unique relationship between the speaker and the listener. If a speaker is talking to a group, then she's suggesting that she has this with *each* person in the room.

"Every" means, well, *every* one in the room. All. None left out. Every doctrine, race, nationality, educational level, income, marital status, station in life, and job.[14]

And maybe if we also accept that believers are somehow mysteriously connected to each other through Jesus and his Spirit, then "each and every one" can become "each and every; one." Each individual, every individual, made one in Jesus.[15] Now *that's* Church.

When someone smiles at a group of people and says "eachandeveryone," I get depressed. It reminds me of how shallow it is, and how deep it's meant to and can be. It's not just the televangelists, really; it's all of us. But the good news is that we don't have to live that way.

The Last, First

I was spending a long weekend with a former protégé in Auburn (the first of many weekends and protégés, as it turned out). A local parachurch ministry, Auburn Christian Fellowship, was about to demolish a building and build a new one in its place. So what to do? Why, airsoft capture the flag inside the old house, of course! We're hanging out while other students arrive, and eventually there are about 20 people on hand for this little episode of spontaneous warfare. The time came to choose teams, and a funny thing happened.

After a few minutes in a group, it's pretty evident who is socially gifted, less-gifted, and downright awkward or shy. It was obvious that night. Perhaps it's easier to see for those of us who were picked last, or picked upon, or just not picked at all.

The gifted ones called out the awkward ones. "Michael, come on over here, be on my team." *All* the gifted ones did that.[E] The awkward ones looked surprised...they'd learned their schoolyard lessons well.

The game commenced. I sort of expected the less-outgoing ones to be sort of ignored as we planned and executed our assaults and defenses. But that isn't what happened at all.

We were all players that night.[F] The leaders weren't just posing their interest in "the last and the least of these." [16] It was real; it happened in the heat of battle, so to speak. We shuffled sides and played again, and again. And it happened, every time.

You see, those young men internalized and personified a key element of leadership in *ekklesia*. The goal wasn't to win, or to see which team member could arrive first. The goal was to arrive together. We accomplished that by putting the last ones first.[17] Like Jesus talked about. It may sound strange to some, but it was church. That night, we were Church.

Who are "we?"

"There is neither Jew nor Greek, there is neither slave nor free man, there is neither male nor female; for you are all one in Messiah Jesus."
   – Galatians 3:28

There's a store near our old home in Huntsville called Unclaimed

---

[E] Just trying to look good, right? Not so fast; read on.

[F] I still cherish the picture of my face, in t-shirt Ninja garb, with blood streaks from a little-too-close battle for control of the hallway. Livin' the life!

Baggage. They buy unclaimed baggage from the airlines, sort out the goods, clean things up, and sell them. There's lots of good stuff; my iPod came from there. The "unclaimed" baggage becomes claimed. Like recycling...or redeeming. "Redeem" is one of those loaded words. It means to buy something back. Or some*one*. Buy back someone that was unclaimed, in debt, or slavery—but just as intrinsically valuable as everyone else.

Jesus walked around the land of Israel claiming and redeeming a lot of people who were marginalized, rejected, discriminated against, hated, outcast, unseen, ignored, sick, and foreign.[G] Ever since, he's been walking into all sorts of places to all sorts of people in all sorts of situations, and saying, I created you, I love you, and I want you to return to me. He built, and is building, a church out of unclaimed baggage. Us.

Jesus told the story of a man who planned a great banquet and invited many guests. But, one after the other, they all found other things to do ("excuses"). Then the owner of the house became angry and ordered his servant, "Go out quickly into the streets and lanes of the city, and bring in the poor, maimed, blind, and lame."[18] I can just see the servant trotting up to every bum, whore, burned-out businessman, and perfect stranger he could find to fill the hall as his master had instructed. I think Jesus must feel like that master but also like the servant seeking those who come from all walks and failings of life.

What if the "we" in our *ekklesias* were the product of the people who are actually here, instead of subject to a predefined set of doctrines and customs defined by the ones who showed up last week, or last year, or decade or century?[H]

[G] Scripture identifies fishermen, Nazarenes, Galileans, Samaritans, tax collectors, prostitutes, lepers, mistresses, divorcees, blind, lame, and "ritually unclean" people.

[H] I'm not saying we abandon the Bible as a standard, or its historic doctrines. That would make the whole enterprise like a room full of direction-*(contin.)*

What will happen when "they"—others unlike us—become "we?"[19]

Becoming Real

How do we wrap up this conversation about who we are, who "we" are, and who we are becoming? Perhaps a children's story is the way to rediscover our hearts.

The Velveteen Rabbit is the story of an ordinary little stuffed rabbit that belonged to a Boy who had many toys. Sometimes the fancy toys made fun of the little rabbit:

> ...the poor little Rabbit was made to feel himself very insignificant and commonplace, and the only person who was kind to him at all was the Skin Horse.

> The Skin Horse had lived longer in the nursery than any of the others. He was so old that his brown coat was bald in patches and showed the seams underneath, and most of the hairs in his tail had been pulled out to string bead necklaces. He was wise, for he had seen a long succession of mechanical toys arrive to boast and swagger, and by-and-by break their mainsprings and pass away, and he knew that they were only toys, and would never turn into anything else. For nursery magic is very strange and wonderful, and only those playthings that are old and wise and experienced like the Skin Horse understand all about it.

> "What is REAL?" asked the Rabbit one day, when they were lying side by side near the nursery fender, before Nana came to tidy the room. "Does it mean having things that buzz inside you and a stick-out handle?"

> "Real isn't how you are made," said the Skin Horse. "It's a

---

less people on roller skates pushing each other around. What I am asking is, just how amazing would it be for us to find out who "we" are *in fact*, not just in our outward assertions and pledges? Jesus and his words to the unclaimed ones around him look a lot more like his words to us when we find out just who "we" are.

41

thing that happens to you. When a child loves you for a long, long time, not just to play with, but REALLY loves you, then you become Real."

"Does it hurt?" asked the Rabbit.

"Sometimes," said the Skin Horse, for he was always truthful. "When you are Real you don't mind being hurt."

"Does it happen all at once, like being wound up," he asked, "or bit by bit?"

"It doesn't happen all at once," said the Skin Horse. "You become. It takes a long time. That's why it doesn't happen often to people who break easily, or have sharp edges, or who have to be carefully kept. Generally, by the time you are Real, most of your hair has been loved off, and your eyes drop out and you get loose in the joints and very shabby. But these things don't matter at all, because once you are Real you can't be ugly, except to people who don't understand."

"I suppose *you* are real?" said the Rabbit. And then he wished he had not said it, for he thought the Skin Horse might be sensitive. But the Skin Horse only smiled.

"The Boy's Uncle made me Real," he said. "That was a great many years ago; but once you are Real you can't become unreal again. It lasts for always."

God, our creator, is making us Real. He's inviting us to participate in becoming Real, and in helping the other Toys to become Real. And it lasts for always.

Next...

Real is as contagious as we let it be.

Mathetes

Spirit-Learner

"Go, and make disciples of all nations..."
  — Matthew 28:19

Mathetes (ma-THAY-tays; plural *mathētai, ma-THAY-ty))* is usually translated "disciples", but its root word means "learner." Christians are called to make learners, which isn't at all the same thing as just teaching.[A] What if the foundation of becoming a learner were relationship, not information?[B]

When my early mentor, Chris, worked on his motorcycle, he put the wrench in my hand and showed me where to turn it, how hard, and why. Then we worked on *my* car. He taught me about ballistics, gunpowder, experimentation, record-keeping, and machining. Then we went shooting. The same grease ended up under both of our fingernails. He challenged me with questions as we went—not only what he had shown me before, but open-ended questions like "What do you think we ought to do next?" He was the father I didn't have. He loved me with a father's love; he still calls me his second son.

I became a *mathetes*, a learner, under Chris. It was a transformation

---

[A] Millions of Christians have been taught that the emphasis of their faith is their "Great Commission" to convert people and teach them about the faith. But the emphasis in that scripture is actually on the making of disciples, learners, which is a much larger, messier and costlier business than "convert and teach."

[B] The apostle Paul repeatedly refers to his mathetes Timothy, Titus, and Onesimus as "sons."

I *chose*. Chris could have "taught" me stuff forever, but knowledge wouldn't have made me a learner. People can be forced to learn information, but no amount of coercion can produce the motivation and inspiration to become a learner.

What if the Holy Spirit, not people, was our teacher?[1] Or if people "taught" and inspired us through the medium of the Spirit that lives within us?

Dust

Rabbinical discipling, what Jesus did with his *mathetai*, means a relationship, huge amounts of time, and walking through life together. It's common for disciples then and now to follow their rabbis for years. Literally follow. An old Jewish proverb says, "Follow a rabbi, drink in his words, and be covered with the dust of his feet." The idea was and is to learn "the way" (to walk, to do, to live, to think, to learn) experientially from the rabbi, which is why the early Christians called their faith "the way."

We "learn" our ways by following, although not so dustily as then. Look at people in high school "learning" (acquiring by trying out) the ideas, styles and swagger of their ways from peer and older models: goth, jock, beauty, freak. In college, the same: architect, Greek, farmer, geek. People in careers, the same again: janitor, baker, salesman, teacher. We pattern our lives after others in the clan to which we aspire.

A lot of it's about acceptance. A lot of it's about longing to become and do those things God built into our image-of-God hearts. It involves learning by watching, trying things on, trying them out, wearing them to see how they fit, discovering who we are, and adjusting our expectations. It's frequently frustrating to discover that "my dream" wasn't really my dream; it was just someone else's dream for me. It's heartbreaking to discover which dreams are unachievable. But then there are the "I was made for this!" moments.

Jesus calls us to try on his ways and to get dusty with him in the business of life. There are no useful examples in scripture of lone-wolves getting dusty with Jesus. What we find instead is groups of people following hard after Jesus, making their mistakes with him and each other, learning along the journey. After all, Jesus called his disciples and followers out from their jobs and homes into an *ekklesia* of disciples. His *mathetai* were literally called out of their previous lives and called into a dusty lifetime walk. Now, as then.

Matt, pastor of the church I attended while a teenager, taught me the heart of a pastor. Matt chose a few of us—I've never known how—to sit with him on the steps at the altar once a week after school and talk about God and us. Matt was intimate and accessible; he humanized the difficult role of pastor into a place of warmth and joy. He showed us God's unconditional love for us and brought intimacy into a place normally reserved for "high church." He was Jesus in action to us. Worship around him was contagious; he couldn't sing a lick, but he had joy. He dusted us with Jesus' dust. He discipled us.

Matt wasn't perfect, of course. But he showed us that being called out and being in relationship together was deeply woven into our learning about life, God, and each other. Like Jesus, he chose us and walked with us.

People choose to become learners because they want to become like someone else. We wanted to be like Matt. Why would a person want to become like a distant teacher? But how irresistible is a learner-maker?

Jesus didn't tell Christians to make more Christians (the word wasn't even invented at that point). He told Christians to make more (dusty) followers of himself. We'd hope that "Christian" and "follower" were the same thing, but really...

Learner/mentor

As I think of the greatest mentors I've learned from, they all seem to be inquisitive, curious, exploring, and experimenting people. It wasn't just about their chosen professions, it was everything in life.

Matt's response when I asked, as a new acolyte, how to serve communion? "We'll play it by ear."

My favorite professor's response, putting down his guitar, when I asked about doing a hardware project for credit? "Sure, whatcha got in mind?" (He really wanted to know.)

Chris's response when I proudly opened the hood of my new Ford Mustang? *"(Grunt, pointing at the turbocharger)* What's that?"
"That's the turbocharger; 40 more horsepower!"
Another grunt and he shook his head (hidden smile). "Something else to go wrong."[c]

Joshua, my history teacher in middle school and Latin teacher in high school, was a dork. He was awkward, short, unstylish, and had the unattractive but amusing habit of blowing his nose in class with a huge cloth handkerchief and inspecting the results. We egregiously disrespected him in and out of class. But I've never met a more aware, inquisitive and conversational man. He was really, really interested in the world around us, and invited conversation, debate, relationship, and dialog. He loved students. We weren't that lovable, I think, but he did. I didn't really appreciate him until after he was gone. I wish I could thank him now.

There was a study by the MIT Sloan management school in the late 90s that looked at predictors of success in young engineers' careers. They found that the most important factor was to have a first boss who consistently focused on the customer and his outside world, not just the product under development. It seems obvious when I write it down, but it isn't quite so apparent in many organizations. It seems that we're like little ducklings, imprinting on the first thing we see moving after we hatch from college. "Mama!"

David was ridiculously brilliant, consistently contentious, and always

---

[c] It was funny as hell at the time. That lesson was important for a young engineer. Especially in, as it turned out, when he went to work on military systems where your edge-of-technology widget may not have to be the very best in combat, but it has *got* to work when you pull the trigger.

open to a new idea. He drove our customers crazy by relentlessly arguing over what seemed like just one requirement among many that our system had to meet. A joke sprang up that he didn't have a watch, because of his complete disregard for other people's time. David really wanted to understand anything that he saw, and was receptive to anything that added to his understanding. Nothing was accepted, everything was challenged, but he made things incredibly instructive. He was a gifted teacher. David was my first boss after engineering school.

Perhaps because he was a learner, he almost always came at the world from a different point of view than the rest of us. It took a while, sometimes weeks or months, before we all grasped what he was driving at. And David usually turned out to have been the wisest of us all.

David set me up for Andy , who drove even more people crazy. Andy wasn't nearly as combative as David ; he just set a heading and started out. Relentlessly, when confronted with an immovable object along his path, Andy would dig in (no retreat!), explain his position, and eventually the immovable object moved. Or Andy found some way around it that eventually led back to his original heading. Some people (the ones wedded to the status quo) called him a schemer. Well, engineering is never status quo; it's always about improving something. If it isn't improvement, it's just maintenance.

I worked closely with Andy for a number of years. Behind the relentless advance was a whole back office learning environment. He was a master of teaching through questioning. It was years before I realized that half the time he didn't have the answers either; he just let people think he did. Somehow, our belief that there *were* answers helped us find them.

What's poured into us becomes what we can pour out into others. It overflows naturally only if we remain listeners and learners. If we think we've learned a lot, we may spout knowledge, but it doesn't matter without the follower's walk.

Even Jesus was a learner, of sorts, and he told us why the greatest teacher simply follows the one who taught him. "Whoever believes in me, believes not in me, but in him who sent me. He who sees me sees him who sent me...For I spoke not from myself, but the Father who sent me, he gave me a commandment, what I should say, and what I should speak. I know that his commandment is eternal life...I speak, even as the Father has [told] me..."[2]

Right after he said that, this learner/learner-maker washed his disciples' feet before their last meal, the Passover meal, together. Then he told them, "do like I did," just as he'd been telling them for three years to walk in his way.

We were made for this, to learn life and pass it on. All life forms on earth have some ability to physically reproduce themselves. We alone have the ability and the desire to reproduce our hearts in others. Only we can pass the dust of those whom we followed on to the next generation. If we follow Life, we leave Life in our wake, perhaps even for generations to come.

Rafiki

One incredibly important role of the people in the Church, for all its learners young and old, is to be Rafikis. "Rafiki" is the Swahili word for "friend."

In the movie *The Lion King*, the young Simba (whose name means "lion") believes that he caused his father, Mufasa's, death. He's depressed and discouraged. A crazy baboon named Rafiki says, "I know who you are!" He takes young Simba into the dark woods with the promise to show Mufasa to him. There, Simba looks into the water at...his own reflection. Crestfallen, he turns away.

But Rafiki points him to the water again, teaching Simba to look and truly see. Simba learns that Mufasa lives in him; he is, after all, the child of the king. He learns to remember who he is.

You see, Mufasa isn't just a name; it's the Manazoto word for "king." Rafiki showed young Simba that he was born royal, born to be king, and that he is *now* the king; he just hadn't stepped up onto his throne. He's the new Mufasa.

A friend reminds you of who you are, your identity, even when you've forgotten or don't know who you are. A friend reminds you of *whose* you are; a child of the king, *imago dei* and a royal heir. A friend accepts you and loves you, and challenges you to be everything God designed you to be. As mathetai, we desperately need Rafikis in our lives. We need our disciplers to be Rafikis, especially in these virtually-fatherless generations.

In the Wild

Some plants are "hothouse plants." They can only live and thrive in one of two environments: their natural circumstances, or a simulation, hothouse, contrived to replicate those circumstances of light, humidity, soil and so forth. Orchids, for all their beauty, must be kept in a fairly narrow (and warm) temperature and humidity band. They are, after all, a jungle plant.

Others are more versatile. Pine trees, potatoes and the humble cabbage come to mind. Every plant has a natural environment. A native hothouse plant would be an oxymoron.

Some of us thrive in very specific social and work environments, others in more variegated (I'm constantly surprised by the number of different jobs people I've met have had here in Florida, as contrasted with the straight-line careers of engineers in the aerospace world I came from). We eventually arrive at a perhaps-uncomfortable balance with our "natural" environment. What *isn't* a natural environment is a brick and mortar classroom; the classroom is just where we are "hothoused" into a social/work environment.

All of the believers we hear about in the Bible are out in the real world: shepherds, farmers, fishermen, tax collectors, and tentmakers. None of Jesus' disciples, for example, had any advanced religious education; they just followed Jesus for 3 years.[3] Their Christian-teaching education is what's mostly recorded in the Bible. But they're out in the marketplace a lot. Rabbinical traditions of the time suggest that they weren't wandering in the wilderness all that time; they were living with extended family groups. They do the teaching/learning thing, but a whole lot more life application.

Things are different in the wild.

In all of the sciences, you need some teaching on the theory: chemistry, physics, and biology. Hydrogen plus oxygen yields water plus energy. But there's a *world* of difference between knowing that and hearing the "pop" as they combine.

Predicting the impact point of a ball rolling off the edge of your table is a matter of assuming a velocity and height, then computing two simple equations. But you only *know* what ballistics means when the ball lands in the cup on the floor. The laboratory work is actually where most science was discovered, then systemized.[D]

It just happens that we usually educate using theory then do lab work to demonstrate the theory. When your mathematical model doesn't work in the real world, you improve it instead of cling to it.

Things are different in the wild.

Your appendix, if you still have one, is in the lower-right part of your abdomen. That's where the textbooks all show it.

My mother was an Army nurse during World War II in North Africa and Italy. She saw lots of organs in various states of disrepair. They, uh, don't look like the textbook. Sometimes, that appendix is on the left. Other things are scrambled around—and that's just in healthy bodies. War wounds are worse.

Things are different in the wild.

I graduated from engineering school, went to work, and was promptly surprised at the difference between work and academic problems. In school the homework was with separate subjects, on punched cards, and alone. When I got out, the work was with digital networked radio systems (like an early form of cell/data phone,

---

[D] Yes, there is predictive science, where theory predicts and defines experimentation, particularly in some areas of physics. But the cornerstone of science is that the two inform each other.

but jam proof), computer terminals, graphics, and working with lots of people who were, um, unlike me.

Things are different...you know.

In the Tame

John Wimber was the guy who started the Vineyard movement in the 1970s. Early in his learning about Jesus, he read a great deal of the New Testament writings on what Jesus did and said. There's an often-told story that he and his wife visited a local church, and after the service, John spoke with the pastor.

John: "So, when do we do the stuff?"

Pastor: "The 'stuff'? What 'stuff'?"

John: "You know that stuff in the Bible, like healing the sick and casting out demons. The stuff!"

Pastor: "Oh, we don't *do* the stuff. We *believe* they did it back in biblical days, but we don't do it today."

John: "I gave up drugs for this!?"

He had encountered a common species of Tame Christianity. So he left the tame crowd, shared Jesus and life with people, acquired hundreds of followers, and did the stuff. Thousands of lives were changed. Not by hothouse, textbook, indoor, institutional Christianity, but by God being allowed to do the real thing: outdoors, one-on-one, on-the-fly. The real stuff.

Things are different in the wild.

I had my own kind of Wimber moment, but not so quotably. I re-read the book of Luke a few years ago, and was shocked at the interweaving of Jesus' teaching and miracle-working. It shouldn't have been shocking, I suppose. Luke was a Greek physician, a scientist of his day, a trained observer and healer. He recorded what he saw in the books of Luke and Acts. Being me, I got angry. Why wasn't I taught this? I'd been taught Jesus' Tamed teachings from boyhood, but no one ever, *ever* taught me that the *way* Jesus did it was teach, heal, teach. Miracles everywhere!

Oh, the Presbyterians and Methodists taught us what he did "back then," and they taught us to pray in the present. Never was it whispered that he told us to do as he did and what that included. I guess they were afraid we might explode or become charismatics or something. Really, though, they were just being very modern and rational. The inexplicable could not be admitted into the room for fear that it would upset well-organized, Tame theologies. Or theologians.[E]

Ironically, the Methodists were the charismatics of the early and mid-1800s, with a highly-decentralized, non-professional lay ministry.[4] They shot from 3% "market share" of churchgoers to 34% in America from 1776-1850, and have been level or in decline ever since.[5] Why such growth? Charles Chaucer Goss summarized it in 1866, begging his peers to reclaim the thriving gospel they had already forsaken:[6]

- Preach to the heart, not just the intellect.
- A preacher should come from the people, "from the workshop...mingling with his fellow man."
- Use plain, common sermon language.
- Set an example as a minister by greater personal sacrifice, such as their constant mobility.
- Ensure "free seats" for everyone; no pew rental or selling of any kind.
- Hold frequent revivals.
- Encourage extremely active non-ordained members, the lack of which would be "fatal." [F]
- Go to new places that need the good news of Jesus, some-

[E] Ever notice the oxymoron wired into combining "theo" (God) with "logy" (logic/knowledge)?

[F] Not just then. Dependence on clergy is on the rise again. Baptist Press News, *Tracking trends: An interview with George Barna,* http://www.bpnews.net/bpnews.asp?ID=17436, Jan 14, 2004.

times even where opposed.
- Remember that being improved by God can only, and must be experienced inwardly and lived outwardly by all.

By the time that list was written, the viral spread of the gospel was Tamed by the Methodist leaders. Clergy were required to go to seminaries, which sprang up like toadstools; all under very firm, hierarchical managerial control (the generic church word is episcopal). Clergy were allowed and then encouraged, to stay longer in fixed locations. The power of the ordained organization grew vis-à-vis the non-ordained. Pews were sold and rented like moneychangers' tables in the temple, mocking "free salvation."

Things are different in the wild. At a personal level and at an organizational level, when we start to systematize God's ways and predict his miracles in people's lives, from salvation to healing, we risk returning to the hothouse. So, let's keep our "discipling" out there, someplace wild, and free, as in, "Stand firm therefore in the liberty by which the Messiah has made us free" [7] No rent-a-pews, please.

Dressed

The Bible talks of being clothed pretty often. It's usually an outward sign of something, like a purple robe for royalty, or clothed with Jesus for right-standing before God. We need physical clothing, but we also need some figurative clothes like humility, conscience, and wisdom.

The Latin verb for "to clothe" is *investare* (in-vest-AR-ay). From it, we get the English word "invest," as in, put money into a business expecting more money in return. We also get the words *investiture*, *investment* and *invest*, all meaning to endow someone with a position, title or authority. The investiture of a king in England is a huge ceremony; in it, his authority is proclaimed, subjects declare their loyalty, and he's invested with his authority, robe and crown.

Being a learner, a *mathetes*, is all about being clothed with knowledge and attitudes, with information and inspiration. We come into this world naked of physical clothing, but also naked of those other, in-your-soul things. We deeply depend on others to invest in us, with their love, their knowledge, and their perspective. Done well, this kind of investiture gives us an identity, a heritage and a future. We tend to pass those things on.

The very best learner-makers among us not only give us clothing of identity, heritage, and future, but they also draw out the beauty God put in us. And we, after all, were conceived *Imago Dei*. They show us that, although born with naked souls and having been taught shame from birth, a Christian can walk through life *un*-ashamed of their nakedness. Many of us have been taught that we remain drenched in shame for life. But God calls us *friends*.[8] Now that is so outrageous it can't possibly be true. Except that it is.[9]

Each of us is a strange and wonderful tapestry of dreams and pains, gifts and disabilities. That tapestry should not be hidden away anymore, because it is acceptable, in fact laudable, in the eyes of God. His inspiration, breathing-into, makes it so. The essence of learner-making is to see those threads, compliment and complement them with God's written words, and clothe them in love and prayer.

There will be stains and sinful threads in our tapestries like the hulls and dirt in a fresh-picked cotton boll. But a learner-maker who looks at the learner with the eyes of God will see the beautiful design and long, like God, that it be fully real-ized. Long that the learner, like the Velveteen Rabbit, become Real. With human encouragement and companionship, the Spirit-inhabited tapestry can be transformed, cleaned and dyed into its full beauty, without blemish, by its Weaver. "The glory of God is man fully alive."

Turning the wrench

We went to one church in which the lead pastor was the one in the pulpit every Sunday morning and evening, plus another hour and a half on Wednesday. In six years we saw an under-25 face twice. There was a problem. And it seemed that everyone was just fine with it.

In 2004 the soon-to-retire president of Lifeway Resources, Jimmy

Draper, hurled the gauntlet on the table, first at the annual Southern Baptist convention, then in a series of "Frog in the Kettle" articles. He somewhat-tactfully said to a gigantic room full of gray hair that young leaders chose to leave their fold for other pastures, because they weren't allowed to "sit at the table."

Sadly enough, 5 years later there's still a debate going on in those ranks over "are we really losing young leaders?" As if "not losing" were ok, when the whole point is to keep and grow them. Draper put his finger on it. As Pogo the comic-strip character said, gazing at the litter all over the forest, pickup-stick in hand, "We have met the enemy, and he is us."[10]

Christianity is fundamentally a "spread the word" religion (I like the word "centrifugal," as in expanding around a center of rotation). When we get in the way of our own message, there are three options to fix it: follow, lead, or get out of the way. Preferably, all three: follow Jesus, lead others, an get out of our own way. Then, when we encounter evil, we have a better and legitimate stand: "We have met the enemy, and he is ours." [G]

When Chris put the wrench in my hand; when Matt said "We'll play it by ear"; when Andy prayed barefooted for me in his office; and when David told me to brief a hundred people on my simulation work at age 23...they clothed me. They were *mathetai*-makers.

"Doctrinal purity" and "quality of teaching" have a place, but are easily made into fool's-gold cages. They *must not* overshadow the importance of creating participative *learning* (not teaching) environments. We desperately need places, people, and situations where new ways are experimented, where people participate, try and fail but are encouraged throughout, and where it's more about getting there together than one getting there first.

Jesus sent his disciples to nearby villages, two by two, to preach re-

-----

[G] The original quote that Pogo parodied, from a message sent in 1813 from U.S. Navy Commodore Oliver Hazard Perry to Army General William Henry Harrison after the Battle of Lake Erie.

pentance and take authority over evil spirits.[11] "Unschooled men," remember? What was he thinking? Well, he's a learner-maker. Let's do the same.

For those of you who are learners looking for help...seek someone who will put the wrench in *your* hand. Hothouse knowledge leads to pride, incompetence, and hypocrisy. It gives you the appearance of righteousness, but not the substance.

Wrench-turning, muscular Christianity leads to humility, capability, and life. The stuff.

My son, Ian, had a best friend, Daniel. At sundown on September 17th, 2005, Daniel and his grandfather were broadsided on their way to watch a University of Alabama football game at a local restaurant. Both were killed instantly. Daniel was 17 and Ian was 18.

The other shoe dropped the next day when Daniel's mother asked Ian to speak at the funeral. Our youth minister, James , led the awful proceedings for Daniel's part of this double funeral, and one other young man spoke. But what I remember is my own son (yes, he's my son, and you'll just have to take my word on this next part).

He was unbelievable. I haven't ever seen *anyone* with such an anointing at a funeral. He was funny, poignant, inspirational, and personal. He spoke as one who knew and loved Daniel, he knew his audience, and he was healing on that horrible day. You could feel the healing in the room. I could see Daniel's mother, and my God, it was like life to the dead for her to see my boy being himself. James was wonderful; he, too, knew Daniel, knew the audience, knew how to bring God's love to earth that day. But the sight of learner and learner-maker on the same stage was part of the miracle. In the wake of such a tragedy, who would put a disorganized 18-year old in front of 600 people? Well, God would.

I think we all paid dearly for that week of death and anointing. Not just the loss, but the cost of bringing Good News to hundreds in the midst of Ian's first huge encounter with Death. Bringing good news when his own heart was breaking and just wanted to run, or hide. Who would put a disorganized 18-year old kid in a situation where he needed to turn to others for emotional survival, but might not? A youth who might channel his fears into flight? God would. I can't yet "thank" God for that, because I'm a dad. But I understand, because I'm a dad. I know that he allowed my not-so-little boy to have opportunities to choose how to cope with Unavoidable Death with slipped wrenches, bruised knuckles, greasy hands...and Life after Death.

Follow the relationships

I've seen attempts by secular and religious organizations to develop mentoring programs. They all sound good at first. The ones I've seen, however, all seem to founder on the process of pairing up mentors with protégés (I'm not saying there aren't any successes; I just haven't seen any). Selection criteria are chosen, such as physical proximity or professional field, and people are paired up. It should work. Why does it fail?

Such programs are similar to internet dating; they're founded on the idea that common interests will lead to a mutually rewarding relationship. Often it does. But wouldn't it make sense, if possible, to start on the other end of the equation: the existing relationships? If you do, you avoid the whole awkward "um, hi, I'm John, and it says here I'll be your mentor" thing. So what happens when we take existing relationships and choose, together, to let them grow into the development of *mathetai*? Sometimes, something very special. (More on the non-existing relationships in a moment.)

I met Justin in a Sunday evening youth discipleship time. Justin didn't usually do youth events; I don't know what drew him to the small group I was leading (he stayed very busy). He was (and is) one the really anointed young men who are coming up and will, I believe, change the world. That sounds drama-queenish, but I really believe that we're seeing an amazing generation rise up. He was very, very bright and soaked up our material on the Jewish roots of Christianity with wonderful abandon. He loved Jesus and loved people.

He did what high schoolers do to the ones who minister to and love them: he left (they grow up it's part of the deal). He went to Auburn for pre-med, and we saw each other rarely. Until he called one May.

"Hey, I'm home for the summer. I'm shadowing two doctors here, studying for the MCAT, and I wonder if you'd disciple me this summer."

I'm a believer that the development of a learner is a near-peer process rather than a mere teacher-student exchange ("walking beside," *parakletos*-style). I explained this, then, "Yes, I'd love to meet regularly with you this summer. My privilege!" We met and talked about God, life, and so forth. (It really was a privilege. Ain't it great to be around promising students?)

Some months later: "John, you've gotta come down to Auburn after school starts and stay a weekend with me and the guys. You'll love it!"

Well, I was still working full-time, and I didn't listen as well as I should have. It was a good year or so before I finally took him up on it—the last April of his senior year I went in Auburn, 200 miles from Huntsville.

He was right. Remember the airsoft story? It was that weekend. Late nights hanging out with the guys, playing Halo, watching videos, chowing down, and worshiping with other people at ACF...good times. God was there in a huge way.

When it was time to go back to Huntsville, two of the roommates, Robert and Joe, said, "Hey, this was fun. Justin's leaving, but come on back. We'll be here this summer."

I did. This time, I brought along another *mathetes*, Ryan, who planned to start Auburn in the fall (I did *not* want him to show up and get lost in the August herd; I desperately wanted him to have *someone* who knew his name and cared about him). It was another incredible weekend: late nights, Ryan out on a horse research project God just "happened" to put in our path, and hanging out. Just anointed. What a way to launch a Godly young man on his career!

Over the next two and a half years, I went to Auburn 17 more times (then we moved to south Florida, which is mostly out of range of Auburn...but that's another story). I joined their Bible studies, their worship, and their play. I laughed myself sick with them, and I cried with and over them. They kept saying, come on back, see you next month. And I found life there with those young people. Jesus came to give us abundant life.[12] I found that *I was made for this*.

Justin led to Robert and Joe and Mike. Robert and Joe led to Brandon, Will, Nick, Jessica, Ashley, Amanda, Anthony, Jonathan, and Kevin. Jonathan led to Brian, Eric, Kyle, and Jennifer. A bunch of those people led me to Jason and Laura, the parents of Joe and Jonathan. Jason and Laura led me to Thomas. Ryan led to (another) Robert. Steven dropped in out of nowhere, it seemed. And all the while, I wasn't trying to do anything. No one was pairing any of us up. God just used each relationship to bless his people, sometimes for a little time, sometimes for more. It was *good*.

What if I'd just written that trail of relationships off as too distant? Well, in this case, I don't think that anyone would have died as a result. But, and this is a huge "but," there are young people out there who are dying for a discipler.

There are children who live in South Africa but have no parents to speak of. They just sit in the front "yard" of wherever they live. They're called "yard children." God help us, we have innumerable spiritual yard children in high schools and colleges across America. I do *not* believe that God predestined those young people to abandonment. I believe, instead, that there are far too many of us who refused God's pleas to come with him to those countless *mathetai*-in-waiting. When we fail to follow the relationships God entrusts us with, we may imperil someone's very life. Someone who needs *us*. Someone who is spiritually poor, hungry, and naked. [13]

People up in Huntsville said, "Oh, how nice that you travel down there to minister to the students." Minister *to*? That would be condescending and not at all what God was doing down there on the Plains. I brought blessings to them, sure, but my God showered me with so much more, through them. At least from my vantage point. They freshened my eyes in ways that nothing else has ever done.

None of it made a lick of sense. There's a university *full* of students in Huntsville; three, actually. I was physically on the campus of one of them (the University of Alabama/Huntsville) two days a week in my after-Army job in continuing education. Why not there? Why in Auburn, of all places?

Next...

Follow the relationships. They can lead you to places and vistas you can't imagine.

Doulos

Slave

"If I then, the Lord and the Rabbi, have washed your feet, you also ought to wash one another's feet. For I have given you an example, that you also should do as I have done to you."
— John 13:14-15

The word "slave" is *doulos* ("doo-lows," the plural form is *duloi*) in the Greek. It's often translated "servant," which leaves us with the impression that this is a hired "servant." Restaurants call their wait staff "servers" now. *Doulos* is nothing of the sort. A *doulos* is a slave, a chattel, human property, bought, sold, beaten, and blessed at a master's whim.

Jesus washed his *mathetes'* feet, even Judas's, who was about to betray him. Foot-washing was the dirty job done only by slaves. To be a footwasher was to be a human doormat, removing dirt, scum and stink from the streets. Footwashers were unseen, unrecognized, used without thought or consideration: taken for granted.

Unmourned.

Lots of things are called "serving" in Christian churches: cooking, cleaning, preaching, teaching, praying, chaperoning, and singing in the choir. Beyond church, we talk of our elected leaders, such as the President, as being public servants. Members of the armed forces talk about serving.

These are all wonderful outpourings of people's hearts and passions to help and serve and lead others; I thank God for them.

But most of the jobs we frequently call "serving" also involve some degree of position, honor, or respect. We stand when a judge or the President enters a room, for example. Some congregations stand when their leader walks into view.

But that isn't what Jesus is talking about here, is it?

Toilets

"The Lord said to Abram... I will bless you and make your name
great. You will be a blessing."
    — Genesis 12:2b

Slavery was common in Jesus' time. People owning people was
normal, accepted. The Greek word *diakonos* (servant) is used 36
times, and *doulos* (slave) is used 118 times in the New Testament
alone, frequently in the "owning-people" sense of the word.

Remember who he's talking to at the Last Supper? His disciples, his
chosen, called-out ones, the first pastors of his new church. All the
"followers" (the much-larger crowd of additional people who followed Jesus all around) are gone; this is the core group. It's the first
Christian pastors' conference. Within two months,[A] these eleven
will be mighty preachers, teachers, leaders of a new faith, tellers of
a new story of good news. They mostly came from humble origins.
All the other leaders they knew (Jewish and Roman) were on the top
of society and wealth.

Slaves were on the bottom of the pile.

Jesus is telling his pastors to clean the toilets and trash cans in other
people's houses.

I was in a church school building one evening, doing something that
seemed consequential, and encountered nature's call. When I en-
tered the men's room, the school principal, Timothy, was humming
and scrubbing toilets.

He looked up with a cheery smile: "Hi, John, how you doing?"

———

[A] Acts chapter 2 describes the dramatic launch of the new faith, during the
Jewish harvest festival of Pentecost.

"Just fine, Timothy. Didn't expect to find you here."

"Well, you know the janitor doesn't always make it, and so I come down here and do the bathrooms. I think it's a good thing for me; kind of keeps me centered."

Now, the janitor's no-shows were an ongoing boil on the backside of the church, and in fact I was later part of the decision to change janitors. But Timothy never complained.

Did I mention he was also the church worship leader? Centered by...men's and women's toilets.

Jesus is talking about *each* of us, the ministers of his gospel, the "royal priesthood,"[1] loving people by getting really stinking dirty. For the good of others.

Paul, the great builder of *ekklesias*, even strongly suggests that honoring those who seem to be lowly does a lot to prevent division in the *ekklesia*.[2] I can't say I've seen that tried in any organization, secular or sacred. But I'd like to see it tested out among God's people. Maybe I can start by doing it myself, being the change I wish to see?

Maybe we would understand God's Word and our place in his Body better, if we just did a global find-and-replace on that word "servant." Let's make it "slave," so that we don't lose our perspective on what this means to a Christian. In America, it doesn't always mean having your back scarred from the whip, and having your family terrorized and divided for another man's profit (it might, particularly in other countries). It frequently means being taken for granted, ignored, and unrecognized for selfless service to other people. It means being unmourned.

We are blessed to be a blessing. Right from the very beginning when God called a tiny people into nationhood, up to our present day as Christian offshoots of that calling, we become a blessing for someone else. As "little Christs" (the literal meaning of "Christian") we are here "not to *be* served, but *to* serve." [B]

Who, where, what?

We talked about finding *ekklesia* and *mathetai*, Church and learners, by following relationships wherever went. Another way of saying it might be, open up to *ekklesia* and *mathetes*-type relationships as you are going about your usual business. The same idea carries into being a *doulos*.[C] Who and where do you serve? Well, opportunities are all throughout your day.

The real trick is, which ones am I called to be a slave for? You probably run into lots of people every day. No one else can tell you who you're called to. But if you try to answer that question all by yourself, you may end up in some very awkward situations. This is where the things we've been talking about come together very strongly for our benefit.

We're created in the image of God. We have some of his beauty, longings and creative fire in each of us. We are given some forms of *ekklesia*; the people around us. We have been given a Holy Spirit, a *parakletos*, to live inside of us, teach us, counsel us, and generally help us in our walk through life. We may have learner-makers still in our lives. Wouldn't it be helpful to let those resources help us sort out the "who," "where," and "what" of our slavehood?

I've been called to help some people financially. Others with financial needs I only walked alongside. I've cleaned flood damage, installed starter motors, and fixed houses. For others it was huge "sharing life together" commitments. Some, I've served by advising, professionally and personally, in the aerospace workplace. I've shared my knowledge and experience in many ways and places. I've

---

[B] Ouch –*there's* an example that challenges my bank account and calendar. (Matthew 20:28)

[C] Jesus' last words in the gospel of Matthew are literally written "As you are going/having gone, make disciples of all nations..." as though the discipling happens routinely as you live your life. You can even read it, "...all the time..." (Matthew 28:20)

walked right past countless people who were in desperate need. How do I (and we) choose?

The only way I know to sort out those opportunities is by asking God and my wife, and listening to the answer with an open mind and heart. "Check-in" with those who know my heart.

Some churches have stewardship committees, which too often are about passing the collection plate. *Ekklesias* have a better way. "Stewardship" isn't about money at all, it's about letting God use *everything* we are and have: our souls, time, talent, and treasure. It isn't about pooled money for next year's generic budget. It's about what each of us should do or not do with *this* day and *this* dollar and *these* people God has put in front of us.

Un-titlement

"But don't you be called 'Rabbi,' for one is your Rabbi, the Messiah, and all of you are brothers. Call no man on the earth your father, for one is your Father, he who is in heaven. Neither be called masters, for one is your master, the Messiah. But he who is greatest among you will be your servant. Whoever exalts himself will be humbled, and whoever humbles himself will be exalted."
  – Matthew 23:8-12

We love titles. They're on nearly every business card you see. They're on nameplates, doors, marquees, and billboards. We love to see "M.S." or "director" or "certified" after our names or "pastor" or "president" or "doctor" in front. We proudly associate ourselves with the mighty-titled and rightly believe, based on long experience in the world around us, that titles entitle us to special treatment and honors. They confer identity and significance.

Titles are crap.

When I took the titles off my business card many years ago, a friend said, "You need to have them on there, because until people see them, they can't get past trying to figure out what you do." Absolutely true, and...

...exactly the point. I was tired of people assuming they knew who I was and what I did from the misleading titles I operated under. So I jettisoned the titles; I became untitled (yes, I know that's not a privilege everyone has). I knew that it was initially anti-helpful in my marketing role to take that comfort-food title away from a customer. People actually had to watch me and think about me and my role to figure out what I did. The payback was in long-term flexibility to give the customer everything he needed.[D]

When two of his *mathetai* asked to be put in charge, Jesus told them that if they wanted to be great, they had to become slaves. Even he, the *Rabboni*, the great master and leader, didn't come to be served and honored, but to serve and be killed.[E]

There's no organization more in love with its titles than the military. Everyone expects to be called by their title ("Colonel, could I have a minute?") and everyone knows exactly where he stands in that hierarchy. Each rank has clearly delineated entitlements. For example, a Brigadier General expects a flag with a star on it, people to rise when he walks into the room, a driver, a certain-sized house and 100-2000 people who are "his." The title entitles. But a few men rise above their titles.

As a nurse in a WWII evacuation hospital, my mother saw soldiers from units all over North Africa and Italy. Troops have things to say about their officers, especially men recovering from grievous wounds and major surgeries. Seasoned troops know when they're badly led. They know when they're well led.

[D] At the W. L. Gore company, new associates not only choose their titles (if any; they're rare), they choose their positions by literally drifting around looking for where they think they fit. One lady whose customers kept wanting a title put a nice solution on her business cards: "Supreme Commander." Non-incidentally, Gore has virtually *no* hierarchical management.

[E] Sadly, they asked for promotions right after Jesus said, "I'm about to be killed." Where was the "Oh, my God! Oh, rabbi, please say it isn't so!" reaction? Matthew 20:20-28, Mark 10:35-45 and Luke 22:24-27 tell the whole story.

"I've got to get out of here! General Roosevelt needs me up at the front! Please!"

The funny thing is that organizationally, Roosevelt (the son of president Theodore Roosevelt) wasn't "the general;" he was the one-star *assistant* division commander. Not the two-star in charge. But the men wanted to, *had* to get back up to Roosevelt.

Roosevelt was the kind of man that other men wanted to follow. His uniform was usually rumpled. His memory for men, and their parents he'd known in WWI, was photographic. He spent enormous amounts of time at the front with his troops, seeing their war and sharing their food. He ultimately won a Medal of Honor for his leadership of his (and others') men through the confusion and terror of D-Day landings on Utah Beach.

His appearance was unimpressive. His health was poor, he walked with a cane even at age 50, and he died in the field shortly after D-Day of an un-heroic heart attack. But, "I've got to get back; General Roosevelt needs me!" is what my mother heard over and over across the sands of North Africa. Perhaps he took to heart the words of a great captain from three centuries before: "You must love soldiers in order to understand them, and understand them in order to lead them."[3]

General Roosevelt had a star; he was "entitled." But he chose "un-titlement" instead of "entitlement." People know the difference.

You could say he "cleaned toilets" for his country. But in truth, he cleaned toilets for the men he loved.

First Jump

"I wish to have no connection with any ship that does not sail fast; for I intend to go in harm's way."
    – John Paul Jones, 1778

There's a unique and rare type of *doulos*, the servant-leader, who deserves mention: the kind that chooses to be the first to take the greatest risk. Men may seek firsts for glory, but sometimes they also seek them for higher reasons. I met one a few years ago.

We call him "General;" he wears the name unpretentiously, maybe even a little self-consciously. as though still wondering how he ended up commanding thousands of people. He comes across like a professor, the kind of guy you might want to hang around when school isn't going so well. There's a ready grin, a "Hi, I'm John" introduction, a not-in-a-hurry cadence to his conversation. He looks a bit like the chemist he is, complete with glasses, except for that uniform with two stars on each shoulder.

You've seen the old paratrooper movies: Camo-striped pre-jump faces lined up at the door, gentle mushroom canopies floating down to impact brutally among hedgerows and bayonets. In this cool, relaxed conference room General doesn't look like those men. But his 350 jumps make him a part of them and them a part of him.

We talk about our jobs.

When the time had come to live-test the Army's new reserve parachute, he happened to be the commanding general of the development and test organization. He chose that opportunity to don the chute, stand in the doorway, and jump out.

First.

Of course the parachute had been tested on towers, out of airplanes with sandbags, and so forth. Skilled designers and craftsmen worked and worried for years to make it safe, reliable, and effective under all sorts of environmental and operational conditions. He wasn't stupid; he did his homework and learned from the team around him. But there's always that moment when a living soul straps it on, asks a buddy to check his gear, and takes it out the door for the first time.

He explains, in words that might echo generals from Uriah[4] to Roosevelt, "Never ask a soldier to do anything that you're unwilling or unable to do yourself."

That's servant leadership. Leadership means choosing to go somewhere and do something first, undertaking the lonely consequences of that choice. Are life, reputation, and relationships on the line? Or is harm far from the way? ("First" is what distinguishes a leader from a manager. Watch the "leaders" you know, and see if they're actually leaders, or just managers.)

William Bradford wrote of the American Plymouth Bay colonization that "all great and honourable actions are accompanied with great difficulties and must be both enterprised and overcome with answerable courages. It was granted the dangers were great, but not desperate. True it was that such attempts were not to be made and undertaken without good ground and reason, not rashly or lightly as many have done for curiosity or hope of gain."

"Good ground and reason..." to go in harm's way. The general's jump out the door? It went just fine. When the time came to field the new parachute to thousands of soldiers in the Army's XVIIIth Airborne Corps, the first two men out the door were the three-star general and his command sergeant major—the two most-senior men in the unit.

A *doulos* begets *douloi*. A leader begets leaders. They have a lot to do with each other.

Redeemed

Let's wrap this up with two final stories about the life-giving power of being servants, a *douloi*.

Once upon a time, we were part of a Sunday school class that "adopted" a family in a poor neighborhood. The un-foundationed corner of their house had sagged, creating a gap between the toilet and the sewer pipe. The resulting leaks of organic materials rotted the floor, making the bathroom unusable at best and a health hazard at worst.

My job was to fix the floor with a friend, Adam. It took four steps: jack the corner back to level, give it a solid foundation, tear out the old wood floor, and re-deck it with new plywood. Step one: Jack it level. It was a tight fit under the house with only a foot or two of headroom for me, Adam, and two hydraulic jacks. Remember the organic materials leaking from the toilet overhead? We were wallowing in moist, um, soil.

Lying there with the rich odor wafting around me, I realized that I wanted to be here. It was an experiential "learner" moment, a *mathetes* moment. The environment wasn't nice, but I was made in God's image to redeem that bathroom and wash these peoples' feet. Adam and I, we had *ekklesia* there. We were *duloi*.

The family never offered to help; they were watching TV. As far as I know, they never thanked us. It didn't matter. We redeemed their bathroom because we wanted to. Kind of like God sent Jesus to show us the way and accept the punishment for our sins, because they both *wanted* to. Nice thought.

Several years later, I had emergency heart bypass surgery at age 38. We were in a small in-home Christian group (an *ekklesia*) with a lady named Sarah. Sarah was a nurse by profession, but more, she healed souls. We had hours and years of *ekklesia* time, and I'd seen it firsthand.

She kept me company in the hospital after surgery while Cyndi, my wife, took a much-needed break. I was low on blood, tired, and sore. She wiped my face with a warm washcloth. Please take my word, there's healing for the weary in a hospital washcloth wielded by a healer who loves you.

She cleaned our house. She found laundry that needed folding; well, what would you do? (Heck, I wouldn't have thought to look for it!) She folded my underwear.

It's a funny thing, but the intimacies we remember the best are the ones that bless our sometimes embarrassing, sometimes gross, humanity. That was the thing; she didn't "serve" in some subordinate or distant way, but closely and personally. She wasn't humiliated, she was joy-full.

I asked her one time, "What do you like the best about your job?" (She was an eye-surgery nurse.)

"Well, sometimes people come in who are *so* afraid. There's something especially scary about anyone touching our eyes. If they want to pray, I can pray with them. And after we pray, they aren't afraid anymore."

A *doulos* is a redeemer; "redeemer" means "ransom-payer" and "healer," sometimes of bathrooms, sometimes of dirty underwear, sometimes of sick bodies, and sometimes, of hearts.

Next...

That's it for describing four cornerstones of a transformed life (not "*the* four;" who are we kidding? But these will do for now). Redeeming the lost, healing the sick, encouraging the faithful, you know, the usual stuff. Doing what we were made to do, doing things like Jesus did, doing it together, answering his grace with abundant outflow, reaching upward, reaching outward. The usual stuff. Let's talk about that some more, from a little different vantage point.

What now?

"For what is our hope, or joy, or crown of rejoicing? ...you are our glory and our joy."
   — 1 Thessalonians 2:19-20

What Symphony?

In the movie *Mr. Holland's Opus*, Mr. Holland is a passionate music-lover, teacher, husband, and father. And frustrated composer: he dreams of composing and conducting his masterwork, a symphony. The story carries us through his life as he shows his students the power and glory of music. All the while, he is gnawed by frustration and failure; life has happened and passed him by on the journey to his destination.

At the climax of the movie, his hundreds of protégés, his *mathetai*, gather in the school auditorium and show him his "failure."

"*We* are your opus."

Mr. Holland learned that the journey *is* the destination. He learned that "what" he dreamed of was less important than "how" and "who."

I cry during that scene. The idea that those you thought weren't watching recognized you, the idea that you misunderstood the whole thing for a long time, comes mighty close to home. Maybe you cry, too.

We started this book by asking what life might be like if we chose to depart familiar church habits and start living out our identities. Remember, we found a Barna survey which suggested that most Christians in churches just aren't that into Jesus, but that their pastors didn't realize it.

This little book is about the melody of your life, and the symphony of your life with others. *Imago dei, ekklesia, mathetes* and *doulos* each have their chapters, but they aren't really different things. They're only four chords of a much greater work, Life. The day-to-day stuff is part of Life. The miracles are part of Life. The Bible calls it *zoé*, spirit-life. I like that. I hope you do, too.

So how do we move from the ordinary to the extraordinary, from the natural to the supernatural?

Stop

The first rule about holes is, "If you're in a hole, *quit diggin'!*" The second rule of holes is, "You can't get out of a hole by digging a new one." If you're in between the orderly lines of church-people and feeling somehow misfit, then "stop" is a pretty good place to start. You may be the one digging. It may not be that you dug yourself into that hole. You may not be actively digging, but it's a sure thing that people are handing you a shovel.

Is it workin' for ya?

Time is your most-limited, most-valuable resource. So, start making plenty of white space in your calendar (we're going to fill it in just a minute, kind of, so don't get too nervous at the thought of all that "irrelevance" just yet). Embrace the notion that it's *your* calendar, not everyone else's. It doesn't belong to your pastor or your kids' coach.[A]

I know you promised someone you'd show up regularly for a job, family dinners, an hour of prayer and study every morning, improve your education, work on six committees, and your kids' sports/dance/whatevers. All at once. So did I, a few times. You might have taken on some all-consuming hobby, sport, or even ran-domness. You may be stuck in the past or fixated in the future. You may even have the lonely all-white calendar problem (good, you

---

[A] It *does* belong in part to your spouse!

can skip this process and put that thing to work in just a minute).

You may have elaborate reasons and justifications for all that stuff, many quite good: "right," "it's for my kids," and so forth. After all, things are the way they are because they got that way. But are they *all* from God, for you? Not likely, more likely, because you accepted a lot of good ideas with someone else's motivations and passions behind them as if they were your own. Good way to end up with a knapsack full of other people's rocks. Remember the three questions?

- What's that thing in your heart
- Who put it there?
- What are you going to do with it?

Hard as it is to make white space, you'll love what you discover in it.

Start

Decide what it is that you *really* want to do, that'll make you and God delighted with each other. Perhaps try the old prioritization trick: "If I were to die on this day next year, what would I do, or be? And with whom?" That will help you discover who and what you care the most about. It will also show you by omission the things that you can drop.[B]

Listen to God's voice as much as possible. He can and will speak to you all sorts of ways. In prayer, listen more than you speak. He's multilingual and multimedia. You might hear a literal voice, a shout, a whisper, or he might use a feeling, a deep and unexpected emotional reaction, dreams, visions, miraculous words of knowledge and wisdom, friends, music, lyrics, strangers, "coincidences," or miracles. Tune your heart to his, with your own music and language.

"*This* is the day that the Lord has made..." Yesterday is gone, and we

---

[B] ...and exactly who may be offended in the process. This isn't going to be pain-free.

can't relive it or change it. Tomorrow isn't here yet, and we can't live in something that doesn't exist.

Today is the day that God has given you, us. Make the most of it; don't regret tomorrow what you didn't do today.

Joshua was the second great leader of God's people, the Israelites. When they conquered the land promised to them after their Egyptian slavery, he summarized the paths before them. The decision before them wasn't primarily tactical, as we might expect; it was who to worship. He said, "If it seems evil to you to serve the LORD, choose this day whom you will serve; whether the gods which your fathers served that were beyond the River, or the gods of the Amorites, in whose land you dwell: but as for me and my house, we will serve the LORD."[1]

By the way, the name "Joshua" (Hebrew *Yeshua*) is the same as "Jesus."

The Israelites had a 400-year history of slavery, then a miraculous deliverance, to remember. You might have a history, too. Joshua called them to a "whom will you serve" decision. It was a doulos decision. So is yours.

Have you accumulated enough regrets to start a new walk?

Embrace uncertainty and mystery

Uncertainty is being willing to say, "I don't know." Mystery is being willing to say, "I *really* don't know, I don't understand, and truthfully I don't *ever* expect to understand."

Modern "rational" thinking, starting in the 18th Century, intentionally rejected both miracles and mystery. The charismatic revival of the 20th Century re-embraced miracles, sometimes to the point of obsession, but mystery remains an orphan in America. We're uncomfortable with uncertainty.

The first step to embrace mystery is to reject certainty. I'm not saying throw the baby out with the bathwater; the basics of Christianity are still the same. Historic statements of faith such as the Apostles' or Nicene creeds are still "the baby."[c] I'm saying that when we think we know all the questions and answers, our pride is showing.

I personally believe that every word of the Bible was accurately transcribed by people directly from the mind and heart of God (that puts me in the minority among Americans, by the way).[2] But even from my point of view, there's plenty—*plenty*—of room for mystery in the Bible. That's part of what makes it interesting and worth reading. And how much more mystery is there with God than with a single book he wrote?

I'll even suggest that embracing uncertainty and mystery is the beginning of humility. And humility is the beginning of wonder.

I did the math to compute the refraction and reflection angles of light in a raindrop, for the first and second internal reflections. I can draw a diagram, based on that math, of what a double rainbow should look like. But only once in my life have I seen a complete double rainbow; it was a holy moment. *Those* moments are when I know, experience, the difference between knowledge and wonder. Knowledge is like equations, but wonder is like the rainbow. One tells you how it works; the other invites you to feel it's effect on *you*.

"Only wonder comprehends anything."[3] And wonder is what the little child in each of our hearts longs to have with God. Jesus said for us to be like little children. Little children haven't yet become certain; their trust in what they're told, mysterious or not, is part of what's endearing about them. From their vantage point, we can better see God and his higher ways.[4]

Understand what *God* shows you and wonder at the rest. Relax. He'll show you more. Cramming more data into your overflowing inbox isn't going to help anyone.

———

[c] In the end, we *all* take our fundamentals on faith. Even the atheists place their faith in the "seen" things of science, and have faith that there is nothing "unseen." I can't figure out how they explain emotions...but that's another conversation.

Remember

Usually, the secular world around you won't resist you seeing your place with God and life differently. Churches, however... in most churches trying to do new things or do things new way is like trying to sing in a boiler factory, the noise of their industry drowns out our voices.[D] Sing anyway.

Machiavelli said there was nothing more difficult than the establishing of a new system of doing things. I've experienced this proverb more times than I can count, or even want to (work and church; same). Our actions in living new lives produce reactions of suspicion, puzzlement, sometimes active and passive resistance, and, on a good day, wonder. After all, if I change, then I change the world of people around me—not always to their liking. Reactions are real and must be addressed with time and compassion. Resistance is inevitable; conflict is inevitable, *war* with people is optional. Choose to see opposition as a mirror to your face, not a millstone around your neck.

Chances are, your "coworkers" in church will give you odd looks. They may bang their hammers a little harder. Conceivably, they will ask management to stifle the singing so that you can get back to hammering like you're supposed to. Management may tell you to shut up.

Sing anyway. Congregants and clergy in a church haven't been given your life or your day. They aren't the ones with which you share a roof. Most importantly, they don't have permission to peep into your relationship with God unless you invite them.

Like little Simba, remember that you're a child of the king. Besides, isn't there more to life than a boiler factory?

[D] Remember The Preachers' Illusion, where only 23% of church members said God was their top priority but the preachers thought the number was 70%?

Look inside

Stop moving your hands and feet: lose the busyness. Get quiet, quit talking, and silence the audio/visual media noise around you. Consider a "noise fast" for a few days. Consider an out-and-out retreat to some quiet, solitary place.

Look for your heart. Now that you've made white space in your calendar, give it to yourself. Invite God to an appointment where the two of you take out your soul and examine it at leisure. It's going to take awhile, and in a way you'll never be done. But you'll never regret introspection and discovery. Remember, you were made in the image of God, and he has a vested interest in you growing up into that image. So do you (so do we all).

Keep your heart, don't "guard your heart" with fences and walls. A lot of Christians try to do this. To the extent that they succeed, they kill *koinonia* and *ekklesia* and prohibit *mathetai* or *douloi*. In particular, seminary-trained people are often taught to "guard their hearts" from the people around them, especially the non-seminarians.[E] The scripture they are quoting, Proverbs 4:23, is better translated "*keep* your heart," meaning, don't just casually give it away to someone else. Keep it accessible.

In a way, this is what we've been talking about all along: keeping your heart. Letting God shine through it and letting God show you the places where you've stained it or others have wounded it, and he washes it clean. Letting him heal it and transform it. And share your heart in community and discipleship and service.

Finally, consider the "whys" of your discomforts with change. It might be that you discover that you are a less-driven, more contemplative person than you thought. But "doing less" might feel like "lazy." Drivenness is, after all, the honorable addiction in our culture. Take the time to listen to God about where that drive came from and how you can be free from it. You might need to separate

------

[E] No, I'm not making that up. I wish I were.

yourself from other addicts—and there's no shortage of them in our churches. Just remember, God's sheep aren't beasts of burden, and people aren't pack mules.

Learn how you learn

We talked a lot about "fourth wall" teaching, and its contrast with rabbinical discipling and mentoring. But there are lots of learning styles and approaches. Some people learn best via ears, eyes, or by doing things. Some have to fidget or doodle. Here are a few teaching/learning methods I've picked up.

- "Shadow" someone; doctors do this a lot.
- Be a disciple like Jesus' disciples.
- Learn cooperatively with a few other students and teachers.
- Inquire and debate different points of view.
- Show and tell; it's not just for kids.
- Observe and discover: Get out in the world and workplace, do "lab work", go on "field trips", experiment, participate, etc.
- Practice dialog (which is "both/and" conversation, complementing and adding ideas) instead of debate (which is "either/or" conversation, competing and subtracting ideas).
- Learn the formula, the textbook answer. You may need it.
- Learn from surprises, good and bad. Emotional moments are teachable moments, if we let them be.
- Hear and tell stories, parables, jokes, myths.
- Teach. Mentor. You'll learn more than your *mathetai* do.
- Destroy the fourth wall that's keeping you separated, isolated.
- Play. If it works for kids, and we're God's kids...why not? Plenty of learning moments on playgrounds, in games, in simulations.
- Let out the artist-child within you: dance, music, drama, poetry, art, drawing, sculpture, touch, video, building, sports, etc.
- Be careful what you "test" for—we have a tricky tendency to teach (and learn) to the test. The old saying in systems is, "You get what you measure." Too often, that's *all* you get.

"Know thyself."

Look around

Who we are can be practically described by what we choose to see and what we choose not to see. Some civilizations are best remembered for what they ignored, like Germans choosing to ignore a Holocaust in their midst. Some people are best remembered for what they saw, like Mother Teresa choosing to see the untouchables of India.

Practice "looking" as you live your normal life. Stop and really *look* at the people and the physical world around you. Did you just notice that flower? Divert your steps, bend over close, and study it for as long as you want. It might be just a few seconds, or it might be a lot longer. See, smell, touch. Feel the emotion. Maybe even wonder.

What about that server or slave who just took your order at lunch? Was that sadness you saw in her eyes? Joy in her voice? Mischief in his gait? Is there a humanity there you can connect with, perhaps speak with? And by the way, it's amazing how much a little simple caring can mean to someone in a service job. Just being noticed. Just...not some appliance. Just...not taken for granted.

We are quite accustomed to ignoring most of the people around us: the clerk, the taxi driver, the neighbor, the "other." But they, too, were made in the image of God. We're also quite accustomed to seeing other through us/them warlike lenses. Instead of "us" figuratively locking hands to form a closed circle, like the "No Parking" sign, try putting one hand in the center and reaching out with the other. Stay centered, but open. It's a little like choosing to "keep you heart" instead of "guard your heart."

Dr. King said, "We will have to repent in this generation not merely for the hateful words and actions of the bad people but for the appalling silence of the good people. Human progress never rolls in on wheels of inevitability; it comes through the tireless efforts of men willing to be co workers with God, and without this hard work, time itself becomes an ally of the forces of social stagnation." [5] And our own stagnation.

Dwell on these things, drink deeply of the life all around you. Don't be satisfied with mere voyeuristic watching. Go deeper than flaccid Facebook-life. Listen and converse. Interact. Taste the bitter and sweet of another person's perspective and station in life. Give mourning its due time and weight. Laugh as long as you want to.

Forgive "the church"

Henri Nouwen said that the hardest thing to do was forgive the church, in part because the church rarely asks forgiveness.[6]

Whatever "church" has been for you, and against you, can inhibit you. If you let it. "The church," as we see it today, is much more an organization than a living organism. But it's impossible to forgive "the church;" that's too vague. It *is* possible to forgive the individuals who have hurt you. Let them go. Let God and the past have them. Be free. If you have to wail, do so. If you need to go tell them face to face, do so.

One side note: when I've made lists of people who hurt me, I almost always end up with another list: people I've hurt. Some, I just needed to confess to God. A fair number of them, I apologized to personally. Funny thing, most of the time those relationships improved (not all; this isn't some Christian fairyland where all stories end happily ever after).

Release

No man is lazy except in pursuit of another man's dreams. That goes both ways; I'm lazy in pursuit of another man's dreams, and other men are lazy in pursuit of *my* dreams. Most organizations, including churches, are lazy except in pursuit of their own dreams. Let's release those who cling to The Preachers' Illusion, and focus on encouraging the 77% of churchgoers who aren't that excited about God. Even better, let's focus on encouraging the 85% of *all* Americans who aren't that excited about God. Let's let go and turn our eyes and hopes outward, beyond the brick walls, beyond regrets.

Let go of expecting other people to really understand your hopes and dreams. It'll free you from blaming them. You'll be free to dance and sing your dreams anyway. If others get it, wonderful; love them, *ekklesia* with them. If not, love them, but don't give away your dreams. How will God's image of himself, embodied in you, ever be seen if you do that?

Let go of other people's hopes and dreams that you've been clinging to but aren't really yours. That'll free you from blaming them later, too. And free up all the calendar space you need for *your* callings.

Ekklesia

See those people you work with? The people you shop from, sell to, worship with, live near, volunteer with, and serve? Start with them; they may be part of the *ekklesia* God is giving you. Look around, speak out with the voice God gave you, and be available for relationships with your time and location.

You may hear, "Our whole church is just *so* close!" Well, not likely. A wedding, wonderful as it is, isn't the same kind of gathering as an intimate dinner for two or three close friends. Or a honeymoon. People who say this kind of thing may be "telling" you that they don't understand what you're talking about with intimacy, connection, and interdependence.

Similarly, you may hear, "We have small-group ministries." Yes; but are they *ekklesias*? "Small" doesn't necessarily mean "intimate." It's just one enabler, among others. *Ekklesia* means to see and be seen, to hear and to be heard, to accept and be accepted, to understand and be understood. Most of all, it means that *God* is in the house. (Some churches even periodically rotate small-group membership. Guaranteed: not ekklesia.)

Look and listen for signs that God is coalescing a Church and seek your part in it. He might give several to you; or, to say it another way, he might give you, his gift, to several. Are you surprised at the idea you're needed, or need others? Let God show you a bridge over your surprise and doubts.

God is chaos—but not like we think

God is right in our midst, but we don't always see him or his work. Similarly, a person trying to tune in an FM station with an XM radio might conclude, "The radio's broken," or "I guess that station doesn't exist." A caveman might look around a shopping mall and see chaos; he has no vocabulary, history, or cultural context for what he's seeing. So, too, we look around and see something we don't understand and say, "That's not of God," or "That's just chaos." If we fear the "new", we risk imposing assumptions and doctrines on our own creator, although the creator is always greater than the created.

We might be drawn to some very unorthodox partnerships with other people, many of them "non-Christians" or from other denominational backgrounds. We mustn't be captives of our own assumptions, culture, and education. God's already at work with us and in the world around us. A little humility helps us focus more on our own part in God's redeeming work and less on criticizing others'. God does some crazy stuff.

Read the bible with fresh eyes

Since God is bigger than us, even the greatest teachers can only see and share a little bit of him with us. Not only are all teachings and doctrines incomplete, most of it (books, internet, radio) is from people who don't know me and my particular callings and limitations. So, how about if we focus more on conversation with God and reading his letters ourselves, and less on third-person assumptions and materials?

Set aside the denominational and doctrinal lenses through which you see and interpret scripture. Read what it says in the plain text: What does it say? To whom was it said? Where was it said? What just happened, and is about to happen? All those things are hugely important in the scriptures, which were written by and to different people in a different time: Jews, in the Middle East culture, 2000+ years ago, usually surrounded or occupied by powerful enemies.

Again, I'm not saying to jettison all the amazing teaching that's out there. Just don't be a man-follower. It's not who you are.

Walls? What walls?

Drive through any suburban neighborhood, and you'll see all sorts of fences: chain link, "privacy," picket. Walls. Gated communities. What do birds know of the walls we build between houses? Similarly, we needn't admit denominational and other organizational limitations to our lives and ministries. We don't have to argue with them if we disagree. We don't have to limit our resources and partnerships to any particular association or organization. We can simply choose to rise above and beyond such obstacles, living out who we are, with those we're called with and called alongside.

In search of mediocrity

Have many Christians stretched "excellence" beyond "love God deeply" into a people-damaging doctrine? Yes. Americans habitually make it a competition to achieve "excellence." This instantly divides the body into winners and losers, ignoring the rest of the gifts, callings, passions, relationships, and resources already available and at work in the body. "Excellence" as we know it is a killer. Instead, let's take who is already at hand and learn how they fit, synergize, and resonate with others around us. And arrive together.

Give us your unclaimed baggage, your mediocre! (We're not so hot ourselves.) It worked for Jesus, didn't it?

Childhood's End

We left Big Church. Then we were part of an amazing homechurch *ekklesia* and we ministered to everyone from college to nursing home.

Of course, our stories are still being written, by God, others, and us. Sometimes we're reminded that stories have low points in them. Our homechurch *ekklesia* of 5 years ended badly. It felt like the simultaneous death of several good friends and a little civilization. Almost a year went by since the deaths and we had no explanation. "Lord, we did what we heard you saying. Now what? Who's left? Do we fit anywhere?" It was a strange and lonely time. After a lifetime in Huntsville, I came completely disconnected from nearly everyone in town. I never dreamed of being in this situation.

Rather suddenly, on the first Sunday in Advent, 2009, we decided to go look at Florida. Why not? As we advanced through the month, Cyndi started to hear "Clearwater" from God. Uncertain, she didn't talk with me about it, just gave it time to percolate between her and God.

We had no idea what God had for us to do down there. We "planned" to move, leave lots of white space in the calendar, and see what he did with it.

We got as far as Birmingham on a Saturday evening, en route to Destin, which was one of several options we were going to explore. Over supper Cyndi said, "I'd really like to be in church Sunday; is it too late to make Clearwater?"

"Nope."

We took a left instead of going straight, showed up at the Clearwater Vineyard, and were embraced. To put it mildly. God confirmed our "where to go" probably a dozen different ways that week. The phrase I heard from the Lord was "Childhood's end." It was as though the first 49 years of our lives had been our incubator. And now...a world we'd never known was before us. Childhood was over, and it was time to leave the nest. Leave Huntsville. It was exhilarating and scary: adventure, discovery (discovering and *being* discovered), fears about finances and "Are we sure this is God's plan for us?"

Like Abram, we got up and went to a land God showed us. We had no idea what was in it. God was raining down on us, and the last thing we wanted was to put an umbrella between him and us.

He rained grace and provision on us, all through the move. It was like drifting downstream on a fast, deep river; the scenery was changing, but we didn't have to swim a stroke. Money, encouragement, practical helps; we received all those and more.

We met a whole new set of people from that church, the neighborhood, and even a wonderful optometrist. God put us in *ekklesia* with a neighbor. And—if it's possible for Christians to be in *ekklesia* with non-Christians—with another. Then another neighbor. He knit us with several people at the unconventional, conventional Vineyard. We wrecked a few people's days, in a good way. Others returned the favor to us.

We've been living out who we are, serving others, walking together with others, worshiping with others, and mentoring others who have nothing at all to do with the conventional church. An engineering job happened in parallel with all this other stuff, giving me interesting work and people challenges. We've been served and we've learned. Many of our interactions are far from "church" activities. But so far, it's been following the relationships one at a time, wherever God leads them. It's been a kind of adolescence, but without all the drama.

All this after early "retirement" at age 46 and 4 years of consulting and gloriously unconventional ministry. What a ride! I don't know another Christian who has the privilege of living this kind of life (although I know quite a few who could do it if they chose to). It's not all pretty, as I said. But trade it? Never. I can't imagine—it's a horrible thought—what it would be like to be droning along where I was five years ago, "making the big bucks." (They weren't that big— no millionaires in government work. But fat money compared to a whole bunch of people.)

Sometimes, you can buy time. If God opens a door, you buy time by giving up income. It doesn't happen to everyone. Many, maybe most, can't do it. But just how many people are out there making lots of money by burning up the clock of the only lifetime they've been given? How many people are out there standing in lines of Company Men, when there's an entire life and land out there between the lines begging to be explored, discovered, loved, and shared?

David, God's beloved psalmist, wondered, "Where can I go from your presence?" Nowhere beyond God's daddying of us, even out there in the hinterlands. If you have arrived at Childhood's End, wonderful. Go on out into the big wide world God has for you. You can't outrun his love and attention.

The whole Florida thing is crazy. So are the early retirement, Auburn, and homechurch things. But we ignore God's invitations at our loss. So I'll leave you with this thought: if we Christians don't do crazy-seeming things on a pretty regular basis, things that look like the miraculous organism of Christ, how will anyone tell us apart from all the good organizations and companies out there?

Finally...

A new view of God and yourself will inevitably lead to a different way of living. You are limited only by your willingness to search, discover, and dare. Your biggest barriers are in your own soul.

When churches harbor meanness and "not my problem" in their hearts, they make my job harder. I want to overlook that stuff, forgive them and walk on (like God does for me). But anything that I see churches and Christians doing "wrong" might really be a problem in my own chest. It might be that, as Cassius said in *Julius Caesar*, "The fault, dear Brutus, is not in our stars, but in ourselves."

As you and your formerly-misfit *ekklesias* walk into your God-given destinies, you are being built by him into a kind of spiritual house.

This began with seeing God, and continued with helping make him seen by others. You grow with the changes and become the "priesthood of believers." If you have qualms, then consider: could we realistically do any better, than to do what we already know to do? It's time to reclaim—and to re-share—Christianity.

The choice for Life, dear reader, is within ourselves.

Endnotes

Introduction

[1] *Casual Christians and the Future of America,* The Barna Group, May 22, 2009, http://www.barna.org/barna-update/article/13-culture/268-casual-christians-and-the-future-of-america.

Called but not Chosen

[1] Galatians 4:18

[2] http://archives.alabama.gov/govs_list/inauguralspeech.html

[3] http://www.library.spscc.ctc.edu/electronicreserve/read9697/dunsmore/PublicStatementbyEightAlabamaClergymen.pdf

[4] http://www.lib.lsu.edu/hum/mlk/srs216.html

[5] http://mlk-kpp01.stanford.edu/index.php/encyclopedia/encyclopedia/enc_birmingham_campaign/

[6] *Letter from a Birmingham Jail*, Martin Luther King,.http://www.stanford.edu/group/King/liberation_curriculum/pdfs/letterfrombirmingham_wwcw.pdf

[7] *Pastors Rate Themselves Highly, Especially as Teachers*, The Barna Update, Barna Research Group, January 7, 2002.

[8] *Surveys Show Pastors Claim Congregants Are Deeply Committed to God But Congregants Deny It!*, Barna Research Group, January 10, 2006.

[9] *They like Jesus but not the church: Insights from emerging generations*, Dan Kimball, Zondervan, 2007; *Revolution*, by George Barna, Tyndale, 2005; *unchristian: what a new generation thinks about*

Christianity...and why it matters, David Kinnaman and Gabe Lyons, Baker, 2007.

[10] Philippians 3:18

Imago Dei

[1] 1 John 1:5

[2] Daniel 12:3, Philippians 2:15. As an aside, the only other use of that Greek word translated "stars/lights" is in Revelation 21:9-11, and it's a pretty big idea: "[The angel] showed me the holy city, Jerusalem, coming down out of heaven from God, having the glory of God. Her *light* ("brilliance") was like a most precious stone, as if it were a jasper stone, clear as crystal..." We are the bride. We are becoming the new Jerusalem right now, shining brilliantly like stars, like costly stones. Like diamonds.

[3] Psalm 147:4

[4] Genesis 1:3, Matthew 5:14, 2 Corinthians 4:6

[5] Matthew 5:16

[6] John 16:8-11

[7] James 1:25

[8] James 5:13-20

[9] Matthew 5:14-15

[10] Jesus' light, John 9:4-6, 12:45-47; our light Matthew 5:14-16.

[11] The whole story is told in the book of Daniel, chapter 6.

[12] To be clear, salvation doesn't come from evidence; evidence comes from salvation (Ro 11:5-6).

[13] AKA the Seven Blunders of the World, http://en.wikipedia.org/wiki/Seven_Blunders_of_the_World, plus the last one, added by his grandson, Arun Gandhi.

[14] *Against Heresies*, Book IV, Chapter 20, para. 7; Iranaeus, c. 180 A.D, http://www.newadvent.org/fathers/0103420.htm.

[15] John 1:1-5

Ekklesia

[1] See *A Greek-English Lexicon*, by R. Scott, and H.G. Liddell, p. 206; *A Greek-English Lexicon of the New Testament*, by J. H. Thayer, , p. 196]; *Synonyms of the New Testament*, by R.C. Trench, 7th ed., pp. 1-2; and *A Dictionary of Classical Antiquities*, by Oskar Seyffert, , pp. 202-203. http://www.hisholychurch.net/ekklesia.html

[2] Romans 12:5, 1 Corinthians 12 (all).

[3] See Genesis 2:7; *ruach* is also used frequently to infer the breath-life of God in the Old Testament

[4] 1 Corinthians 12:24

[5] 2 Corinthians 9:6-8

[6] Tertullian, Bindley's translation, *Apologeticus* Chapter 39, 1890, http://www.tertullian.org/articles/bindley_apol/bindley_apol.htm.

[7] In his book *The Forgotten Ways*, Alan Hirsch has a wonderful discussion on the effects of architecture on the believers' experience when they gather.

[8] "Fellowship" (*koinonia*) is used in Acts 2:42-47 & "the multitude" (*plethos*) in 4:32-25.

[9] See Mark 3:31-35 and Luke 8:19-21

[10] 1 Peter 2:5a, 9a

[11] For a wonderful parable of our God-given desires, see *The Dream Giver*, by Bruce Wilkinson. (2003)

[12] Memorable one-line picture of the character of God, in sharp contrast to so many other memorable one-liners, courtesy of Jeff Ghiotto, Summer 2010.

[13] The cathedral picture is courtesy of Andrew Jones, a blogger on organic and new expressions of church. June 15, 2006, http://tallskinnykiwi.typepad.com/tallskinnykiwi/2006/06/how_do_you_buil.html, "How do you Build a Cathedral?"

[14] Colossians 3:10-13a "...[we are] being renewed in knowledge after the image of the Creator, where there can't be Greek and Jew, circumcision and uncircumcision, barbarian, Scythian, bondservant, freeman; but the Messiah is all, and in all. [Therefore, beloved, put on] a heart of compassion, kindness, lowliness, humility, and perseverance; bearing with one another, and forgiving each other..."

[15] Galatians 3:28 "There is neither Jew nor Greek, there is neither slave nor free man, there is neither male nor female; for you are all one in Messiah Jesus."

[16] See Matthew 25:31-46 for the importance of this.

[17] From a wonderful allegorical book on system engineering and management, using a Boy Scout hike as a sub-allegory, written as a novel by Eliyahu M. Goldratt and Jeff Cox, *The Goal*, 3rd Ed., 2004, p.

117. Not to mention the Bible: Mark 9:33-37; "If any man wants to be first, he shall be last of all, and servant of all."

[18] Luke 14:12-24 has the whole story. Jesus actually starts out by saying not to invite your friends. Yes, there's a conversational context there, but still, there's a truth for us in there, too.

[19] Rob Bell explores this in beautiful detail in *Sex God*, p. 25.

Mathetes

[1] "...when he, the Spirit of truth, has come, he will guide you into all truth, for he will not speak from himself; but whatever he hears, he will speak. He will declare to you things that are coming." (John 16:13)

[2] John 12:44-45, 49-50

[3] Acts 4:13

[4] The Presbyterians, having briefly embraced the revival sprit of the Second Great Awakening, by 1804 sought to actively suppress any participation in such things as miracles and prophecies. It was said, "These are evidences of a wild enthusiastic spirit, and tend eventually to destroy the authority of the word of God, as the sole rule of faith and practice." God help us.

[5] The *Churching of America 1776-2005: Winners and Losers in Our Religious Economy*, Roger Finke and Rodney Stark, Rutgers University Press, 2008, p. 157. This book covers in exacting detail the rise and fall of Christian groups in the 1800s. The chapter on "The Upstart Sects Win America" is the source for the whole "Methodist" story here, and tells half of the story in the title alone.

[6] *Statistical History of the First Century of American Methodism*, C. C. Goss, Carlton and Porter, NY, NY, 1866.

[7] Galatians 5:1, John 8:31-32

[8] John 15:14-17; verse 15 is the centerpiece of this passage to do what he commands (v14), which is to love (v17). Moses (Exodus 3:11) and Abraham (James 2:23) were also called friends of God.

[9] At conversion we somehow become descendants not of the first man Adam, who started this mess, but of the "second Adam," Jesus himself. And before their first sin, Adam and Eve "were both naked, and they were not ashamed." (Romans 5:12-20, Genesis 2:25, Romans 8:15; Galatians 4:6-7) For a detailed set of Biblical comparisons and contrasts between Adam and Jesus as a type of second and better Adam, see http://www.biblestudytools.com/dictionaries/bakers-evangelical-dictionary/adam-the-second.html.

[10] The original quote was for an Earth Day cartoon in 1970; http://en.wikipedia.org/wiki/File:Kellyposter1970.jpg.

[11] Mark 6:7-12

[12] John 10:10

[13] Matthew 25:31-46. Jesus makes it clear that as we have helped or failed to help the poor, sick and imprisoned, it's as though we've done it to him.

Doulos

[1] 1 Peter 2:9

[2] 1 Corinthians 12:23-25

[3] Henri Turenne, Marshal General of France, 1611-1675.

[4] Uriah was one of King David's generals in Israel around 1000 B.C. When David recalled him from the field, wouldn't even go into his own house and see his wife because his own men were still out in the field fighting a rival nation, the Ammonites.

What now?

[1] Joshua 24:15

[2] *One-Third of Americans Believe the Bible is Literally True*, Gallup Poll, May 25, 2007, http://www.gallup.com/poll/27682/onethird-americans-believe-bible-literally-true.aspx

[3] St. Gregory of Nyssa, AD 335–394+

[4] Isaiah 55:9

[5] *Letter from a Birmingham Jail*, Martin Luther King.

[6] For more on this topic, see *They like Jesus but not the church: Insights from emerging generations*, Dan Kimball, 2007, Zondervan.

www.ingramcontent.com/pod-product-compliance
Lightning Source LLC
Chambersburg PA
CBHW020510030426
42337CB00011B/318